INDEX

Addition of Two 8-bit Numbers

Subtraction of Two 8-bit Numbers

Multiplication of Two 8-bit Numbers

Division of Two 8-bit Numbers

Addition of Two 16-bit Numbers

Subtraction of Two 16-bit Numbers

Multiplication of Two 16-bit Numbers

Division of Two 16-bit Numbers

Addition of Two BCD Numbers

Subtraction of Two BCD Numbers

BCD to Binary Conversion

Binary to BCD Conversion

ASCII to Binary Conversion

Binary to ASCII Conversion

Finding Largest Number in Array

Finding Smallest Number in Array

Sorting Array in Ascending Order

Sorting Array in Descending Order

Counting Number of Ones in a Byte

Counting Number of Zeros in a Byte

Checking Even or Odd Number

Parity Check

Sum of Series of 8-bit Numbers

Sum of Series of 16-bit Numbers

Reverse a String

String Length Calculation

Palindrome Check for String

Fibonacci Series Generation

Factorial Calculation

GCD of Two Numbers

LCM of Two Numbers

Prime Number Check

Prime Numbers in a Range

Armstrong Number Check

Find Square of a Number

Find Cube of a Number

Linear Search in Array

Binary Search in Array

Matrix Addition

Matrix Subtraction

Matrix Multiplication

Transpose of a Matrix

Determinant of a Matrix

Sum of Diagonals of a Matrix

Sum of Rows of a Matrix

Sum of Columns of a Matrix

Bitwise AND Operation

Bitwise OR Operation

Bitwise XOR Operation

Bitwise NOT Operation

Left Rotate a Byte

Right Rotate a Byte

Left Shift a Byte

Right Shift a Byte

Swap Two Numbers

Interchange First and Last Digits of a Number

Calculate Simple Interest

Calculate Compound Interest

Find ASCII Value of a Character

Character to Uppercase Conversion

Character to Lowercase Conversion

Find Power of a Number

Find Square Root of a Number

Decimal to Binary Conversion

Binary to Decimal Conversion

Decimal to Hexadecimal Conversion

Hexadecimal to Decimal Conversion

Decimal to Octal Conversion

Octal to Decimal Conversion

Hexadecimal to Binary Conversion

Binary to Hexadecimal Conversion

Hexadecimal to ASCII Conversion

ASCII to Hexadecimal Conversion

Display Character String

Display ASCII Table

Find Sum of Digits of a Number

Reverse Digits of a Number

Check for Armstrong Number in a Range

Check for Perfect Number

Find Sum of N Natural Numbers

Find Sum of Squares of N Natural Numbers

Find Sum of Cubes of N Natural Numbers

Generate Pascal's Triangle

Count Vowels in a String

Count Consonants in a String

Reverse Words in a Sentence

Count Number of Words in a Sentence

Convert Decimal Number to Roman Numeral

Calculate Body Mass Index (BMI)

Temperature Conversion (Celsius to Fahrenheit)

Temperature Conversion (Fahrenheit to Celsius)

Generate Random Numbers

Simulate Dice Roll

Simulate Coin Toss

Leap Year Check

Display Current Date and Time

Generate Calendar of a Month

Convert 12-hour Time Format to 24-hour

Convert 24-hour Time Format to 12-hour

Display Day of the Week for Given Date

Find Day of Year for Given Date

Calculate Age in Days

Calculate Difference Between Two Dates

Convert Kilometers to Miles

Convert Miles to Kilometers

Calculate Area of Circle

Calculate Circumference of Circle

Calculate Area of Rectangle

Calculate Perimeter of Rectangle

Calculate Area of Triangle

Calculate Perimeter of Triangle

Calculate Volume of Sphere

Calculate Surface Area of Sphere

Calculate Volume of Cylinder

Calculate Surface Area of Cylinder

Calculate Volume of Cone

Calculate Surface Area of Cone

Find Roots of Quadratic Equation

Calculate Sine of Angle

Calculate Cosine of Angle

Calculate Tangent of Angle

Calculate Logarithm of Number

Calculate Exponential of Number

Calculate Absolute Value

Find Hamming Distance Between Two Strings

Check for Substring

String Concatenation

String Copy

String Compare

Convert Integer to String

Convert String to Integer

Implement Stack Operations (Push, Pop)

Implement Queue Operations (Enqueue, Dequeue)

Implement Circular Queue

Implement Priority Queue

Implement Linked List (Insertion, Deletion)

Implement Doubly Linked List

Implement Circular Linked List

Implement Binary Tree (Insertion, Traversal)

Implement Binary Search Tree

Implement AVL Tree

Implement Graph (Adjacency Matrix)

8088 MICROPROCESSOR PROGRAMMING

Addition of Two 8-bit Numbers

```
ORG 100h     ; Origin, start at address 100h
MOV AL, 25h  ; Load first number into AL
MOV BL, 37h  ; Load second number into BL
ADD AL, BL   ; Add BL to AL, result in AL
HLT          ; Halt the program
```

Subtraction of Two 8-bit Numbers

```
ORG 100h     ; Origin, start at address 100h
MOV AL, 45h  ; Load first number into AL
MOV BL, 12h  ; Load second number into BL
SUB AL, BL   ; Subtract BL from AL, result in AL
HLT          ; Halt the program
```

Multiplication of Two 8-bit Numbers

```
ORG 100h     ; Origin, start at address 100h
MOV AL, 08h  ; Load first number into AL
MOV BL, 06h  ; Load second number into BL
MUL BL       ; Multiply AL by BL, result in AX (AH:AL)
HLT          ; Halt the program
```

Division of Two 8-bit Numbers

```
ORG 100h     ; Origin, start at address 100h
MOV AL, 48h  ; Load dividend into AL
MOV BL, 06h  ; Load divisor into BL
DIV BL       ; Divide AL by BL, quotient in AL, remainder in AH
HLT          ; Halt the program
```

Addition of Two 16-bit Numbers

ORG 100h   ; Origin, start at address 100h

MOV AX, 1234h ; Load first number into AX

MOV BX, 5678h ; Load second number into BX

ADD AX, BX   ; Add BX to AX, result in AX

HLT   ; Halt the program

Subtraction of Two 16-bit Numbers

ORG 100h   ; Origin, start at address 100h

MOV AX, 1234h ; Load first number into AX

MOV BX, 5678h ; Load second number into BX

SUB AX, BX   ; Subtract BX from AX, result in AX

HLT   ; Halt the program

Multiplication of Two 16-bit Numbers

ORG 100h   ; Origin, start at address 100h

MOV AX, 1234h ; Load first number into AX

MOV BX, 5678h ; Load second number into BX

MUL BX   ; Multiply AX by BX, result in DX:AX

HLT   ; Halt the program

Division of Two 16-bit Numbers

ORG 100h   ; Origin, start at address 100h

MOV AX, 1234h ; Load dividend into AX

MOV BX, 0034h ; Load divisor into BX

XOR DX, DX   ; Clear DX to ensure no higher bits affect division

DIV BX   ; Divide AX by BX, quotient in AX, remainder in DX

HLT   ; Halt the program

Addition of Two BCD Numbers

```
ORG 100h     ; Origin, start at address 100h
MOV AL, 25h  ; Load first BCD number into AL (BCD 25)
MOV BL, 37h  ; Load second BCD number into BL (BCD 37)
ADD AL, BL   ; Add BL to AL, result in AL
DAA          ; Adjust result to BCD
HLT          ; Halt the program
```

Subtraction of Two BCD Numbers

```
ORG 100h     ; Origin, start at address 100h
MOV AL, 45h  ; Load first BCD number into AL (BCD 45)
MOV BL, 12h  ; Load second BCD number into BL (BCD 12)
SUB AL, BL   ; Subtract BL from AL, result in AL
DAS          ; Adjust result to BCD
HLT          ; Halt the program
```

BCD to Binary Conversion

```
ORG 100h     ; Origin, start at address 100h
MOV AL, 25h  ; Load BCD number into AL (BCD 25)
MOV AH, AL   ; Copy AL to AH
AND AH, 0Fh  ; Isolate the lower nibble
MOV CL, 4    ; Prepare to shift left by 4
SHR AL, CL   ; Shift right by 4 bits to get the upper nibble
ADD AL, AH   ; Add the lower nibble
HLT          ; Halt the program
```

Binary to BCD Conversion

```
ORG 100h     ; Origin, start at address 100h
MOV AL, 25d  ; Load binary number into AL (Decimal 25)
```

```
MOV AH, AL    ; Copy AL to AH
AND AH, 0Fh   ; Mask lower nibble
MOV CL, 4     ; Prepare to shift left by 4
SHR AL, CL    ; Shift right by 4 bits
ADD AL, 30h   ; Add '0' to the result
ADD AH, 0Fh   ; Add 'F' to the lower nibble
DAA           ; Decimal Adjust AL
HLT           ; Halt the program
```

ASCII to Binary Conversion

```
ORG 100h      ; Origin, start at address 100h
MOV AL, '5'   ; Load ASCII character '5' into AL
SUB AL, 30h   ; Subtract ASCII '0' to get the binary equivalent
HLT           ; Halt the program
```

Binary to ASCII Conversion

```
ORG 100h      ; Origin, start at address 100h
MOV AL, 05h   ; Load binary number 5 into AL
ADD AL, 30h   ; Add ASCII '0' to get the ASCII character '5'
HLT           ; Halt the program
```

Finding Largest Number in Array

```
ORG 100h      ; Origin, start at address 100h
MOV SI, 0     ; Initialize source index
MOV CX, 5     ; Array size
MOV AL, 0     ; Initialize largest number to 0
MOV BYTE PTR [SI], 25h
MOV BYTE PTR [SI + 1], 37h
MOV BYTE PTR [SI + 2], 12h
```

```
MOV BYTE PTR [SI + 3], 45h
MOV BYTE PTR [SI + 4], 30h
; Find the largest number
MOV SI, 0    ; Reset source index
NEXT_NUM:
MOV BL, [SI]  ; Load array element into BL
CMP AL, BL    ; Compare AL with BL
JAE SKIP      ; If AL >= BL, skip to next
MOV AL, BL    ; If BL > AL, update AL with BL
SKIP:
INC SI        ; Move to the next element
LOOP NEXT_NUM ; Repeat for all elements
HLT           ; Halt the program
```

Finding Smallest Number in Array

```
ORG 100h      ; Origin, start at address 100h
MOV SI, 0     ; Initialize source index
MOV CX, 5     ; Array size
MOV AL, FFh   ; Initialize smallest number to maximum 8-bit value
; Array data
MOV BYTE PTR [SI], 25h
MOV BYTE PTR [SI + 1], 37h
MOV BYTE PTR [SI + 2], 12h
MOV BYTE PTR [SI + 3], 45h
MOV BYTE PTR [SI + 4], 30h
; Find the smallest number
MOV SI, 0     ; Reset source index
NEXT_NUM:
MOV BL, [SI]  ; Load array element into BL
```

```
CMP AL, BL   ; Compare AL with BL
JBE SKIP     ; If AL <= BL, skip to next
MOV AL, BL   ; If BL < AL, update AL with BL
SKIP:
INC SI       ; Move to the next element
LOOP NEXT_NUM ; Repeat for all elements
HLT          ; Halt the program
```

Sorting Array in Ascending Order

```
ORG 100h     ; Origin, start at address 100h
MOV CX, 5    ; Array size
; Array data
MOV BYTE PTR [0], 25h
MOV BYTE PTR [1], 37h
MOV BYTE PTR [2], 12h
MOV BYTE PTR [3], 45h
MOV BYTE PTR [4], 30h
SORT:
MOV SI, 0    ; Initialize source index
MOV DI, CX   ; Initialize inner loop counter
DEC DI
NEXT_PASS:
MOV AL, [SI]  ; Load first element into AL
MOV BL, [SI + 1] ; Load second element into BL
CMP AL, BL   ; Compare AL and BL
JBE NO_SWAP  ; If AL <= BL, no swap needed
XCHG AL, BL  ; Swap AL and BL
MOV [SI], AL  ; Store AL back to array
MOV [SI + 1], BL ; Store BL back to array
```

```
NO_SWAP:
INC SI       ; Move to the next element
DEC DI       ; Decrement inner loop counter
JNZ NEXT_PASS ; Repeat inner loop if DI != 0
DEC CX       ; Decrement outer loop counter
JNZ SORT     ; Repeat outer loop if CX != 0
HLT          ; Halt the program
```

Sorting Array in Descending Order

```
ORG 100h      ; Origin, start at address 100h
MOV CX, 5     ; Array size
; Array data
MOV BYTE PTR [0], 25h
MOV BYTE PTR [1], 37h
MOV BYTE PTR [2], 12h
MOV BYTE PTR [3], 45h
MOV BYTE PTR [4], 30h
SORT:
MOV SI, 0     ; Initialize source index
MOV DI, CX    ; Initialize inner loop counter
DEC DI
NEXT_PASS:
MOV AL, [SI]  ; Load first element into AL
MOV BL, [SI + 1] ; Load second element into BL
CMP AL, BL    ; Compare AL and BL
JAE NO_SWAP   ; If AL >= BL, no swap needed
XCHG AL, BL   ; Swap AL and BL
MOV [SI], AL  ; Store AL back to array
MOV [SI + 1], BL ; Store BL back to array
```

```
NO_SWAP:
INC SI       ; Move to the next element
DEC DI       ; Decrement inner loop counter
JNZ NEXT_PASS ; Repeat inner loop if DI != 0
DEC CX       ; Decrement outer loop counter
JNZ SORT     ; Repeat outer loop if CX != 0
HLT          ; Halt the program
```

Counting Number of Ones in a Byte

```
ORG 100h     ; Origin, start at address 100h
MOV AL, 96h  ; Load the byte to be counted
MOV CX, 8    ; Set counter to 8 bits
MOV BL, 0    ; Clear the count
COUNT_ONES:
SHR AL, 1    ; Shift right AL
JNC NO_INC   ; If no carry, skip increment
INC BL       ; Increment count if carry is set
NO_INC:
LOOP COUNT_ONES ; Repeat for all bits
HLT          ; Halt the program
```

Counting Number of Zeros in a Byte

```
ORG 100h     ; Origin, start at address 100h
MOV AL, 96h  ; Load the byte to be counted
MOV CX, 8    ; Set counter to 8 bits
MOV BL, 0    ; Clear the count
COUNT_ZEROS:
SHR AL, 1    ; Shift right AL
JC NO_INC    ; If carry, skip increment
```

```
INC BL        ; Increment count if no carry
NO_INC:
LOOP COUNT_ZEROS ; Repeat for all bits
HLT           ; Halt the program
```

Finding Smallest Number in Array

```
ORG 100h      ; Origin, start at address 100h
MOV SI, 0     ; Initialize source index
MOV CX, 5     ; Array size
MOV AL, FFh   ; Initialize smallest number to maximum 8-bit value
; Array data
MOV BYTE PTR [SI], 25h
MOV BYTE PTR [SI + 1], 37h
MOV BYTE PTR [SI + 2], 12h
MOV BYTE PTR [SI + 3], 45h
MOV BYTE PTR [SI + 4], 30h
; Find the smallest number
MOV SI, 0     ; Reset source index
NEXT_NUM:
MOV BL, [SI]  ; Load array element into BL
CMP AL, BL    ; Compare AL with BL
JBE SKIP      ; If AL <= BL, skip to next
MOV AL, BL    ; If BL < AL, update AL with BL
SKIP:
INC SI        ; Move to the next element
LOOP NEXT_NUM ; Repeat for all elements
HLT           ; Halt the program
```

Sorting Array in Ascending Order

```
ORG 100h      ; Origin, start at address 100h
MOV CX, 5     ; Array size
; Array data
MOV BYTE PTR [0], 25h
MOV BYTE PTR [1], 37h
MOV BYTE PTR [2], 12h
MOV BYTE PTR [3], 45h
MOV BYTE PTR [4], 30h
SORT:
MOV SI, 0     ; Initialize source index
MOV DI, CX    ; Initialize inner loop counter
DEC DI
NEXT_PASS:
MOV AL, [SI]  ; Load first element into AL
MOV BL, [SI + 1] ; Load second element into BL
CMP AL, BL    ; Compare AL and BL
JBE NO_SWAP   ; If AL <= BL, no swap needed
XCHG AL, BL   ; Swap AL and BL
MOV [SI], AL  ; Store AL back to array
MOV [SI + 1], BL ; Store BL back to array
NO_SWAP:
INC SI        ; Move to the next element
DEC DI        ; Decrement inner loop counter
JNZ NEXT_PASS ; Repeat inner loop if DI != 0
DEC CX        ; Decrement outer loop counter
JNZ SORT      ; Repeat outer loop if CX != 0
HLT           ; Halt the program
```

Sorting Array in Descending Order

```
ORG 100h     ; Origin, start at address 100h
MOV CX, 5    ; Array size
; Array data
MOV BYTE PTR [0], 25h
MOV BYTE PTR [1], 37h
MOV BYTE PTR [2], 12h
MOV BYTE PTR [3], 45h
MOV BYTE PTR [4], 30h
SORT:
MOV SI, 0    ; Initialize source index
MOV DI, CX   ; Initialize inner loop counter
DEC DI
NEXT_PASS:
MOV AL, [SI]  ; Load first element into AL
MOV BL, [SI + 1] ; Load second element into BL
CMP AL, BL   ; Compare AL and BL
JAE NO_SWAP  ; If AL >= BL, no swap needed
XCHG AL, BL  ; Swap AL and BL
MOV [SI], AL  ; Store AL back to array
MOV [SI + 1], BL ; Store BL back to array
NO_SWAP:
INC SI       ; Move to the next element
DEC DI       ; Decrement inner loop counter
JNZ NEXT_PASS ; Repeat inner loop if DI != 0
DEC CX       ; Decrement outer loop counter
JNZ SORT     ; Repeat outer loop if CX != 0
HLT          ; Halt the program
```

Counting Number of Ones in a Byte

```
ORG 100h      ; Origin, start at address 100h
MOV AL, 96h   ; Load the byte to be counted
MOV CX, 8     ; Set counter to 8 bits
MOV BL, 0     ; Clear the count
COUNT_ONES:
SHR AL, 1     ; Shift right AL
JNC NO_INC    ; If no carry, skip increment
INC BL        ; Increment count if carry is set
NO_INC:
LOOP COUNT_ONES ; Repeat for all bits
HLT           ; Halt the program
```

Counting Number of Zeros in a Byte

```
ORG 100h      ; Origin, start at address 100h
MOV AL, 96h   ; Load the byte to be counted
MOV CX, 8     ; Set counter to 8 bits
MOV BL, 0     ; Clear the count
COUNT_ZEROS:
SHR AL, 1     ; Shift right AL
JC NO_INC     ; If carry, skip increment
INC BL        ; Increment count if no carry
NO_INC:
LOOP COUNT_ZEROS ; Repeat for all bits
HLT           ; Halt the program
```

Checking Even or Odd Number

```
ORG 100h      ; Origin, start at address 100h
MOV AL, 25h   ; Load number into AL
```

```
TEST AL, 1    ; Test if the least significant bit is 1
JZ EVEN       ; If zero flag is set, number is even
; Code for Odd number
ODD:
MOV DL, 'O'   ; Load 'O' for Odd
JMP END
; Code for Even number
EVEN:
MOV DL, 'E'   ; Load 'E' for Even
; End of program
END:
HLT           ; Halt the program
```

Parity Check

```
ORG 100h      ; Origin, start at address 100h
MOV AL, 96h   ; Load number into AL
; Check parity
MOV DL, 'E'   ; Assume even parity
MOV CX, 8     ; Set counter to 8 bits
MOV BL, 0     ; Clear the count
PARITY_CHECK:
SHR AL, 1     ; Shift right AL
JNC NO_INC    ; If no carry, skip increment
INC BL        ; Increment count if carry is set
NO_INC:
LOOP PARITY_CHECK ; Repeat for all bits
TEST BL, 1    ; Test the count of 1s
JNZ ODD_PARITY ; If odd number of 1s, it's odd parity
; Even parity
```

```
EVEN_PARITY:
MOV DL, 'E'   ; Load 'E' for Even parity
JMP END
; Odd parity
ODD_PARITY:
MOV DL, 'O'   ; Load 'O' for Odd parity
; End of program
END:
HLT           ; Halt the program
```

Sum of Series of 8-bit Numbers

```
ORG 100h      ; Origin, start at address 100h
MOV SI, 0     ; Initialize source index
MOV CX, 5     ; Array size
MOV AL, 0     ; Clear accumulator for sum
; Array data
MOV BYTE PTR [SI], 25h
MOV BYTE PTR [SI + 1], 37h
MOV BYTE PTR [SI + 2], 12h
MOV BYTE PTR [SI + 3], 45h
MOV BYTE PTR [SI + 4], 30h
; Calculate sum
MOV SI, 0     ; Reset source index
SUM_LOOP:
ADD AL, [SI]  ; Add array element to AL
INC SI        ; Move to the next element
LOOP SUM_LOOP ; Repeat for all elements
HLT           ; Halt the program
```

Sum of Series of 16-bit Numbers

```
ORG 100h      ; Origin, start at address 100h
MOV SI, 0     ; Initialize source index
MOV CX, 3     ; Array size (3 elements)
XOR AX, AX    ; Clear accumulator for sum
; Array data
MOV WORD PTR [SI], 1234h
MOV WORD PTR [SI + 2], 5678h
MOV WORD PTR [SI + 4], 9ABCh
; Calculate sum
MOV SI, 0     ; Reset source index
SUM_LOOP:
ADD AX, [SI]  ; Add array element to AX
ADD SI, 2     ; Move to the next 16-bit element
LOOP SUM_LOOP ; Repeat for all elements
HLT           ; Halt the program
```

Reverse a String

```
ORG 100h      ; Origin, start at address 100h
MOV SI, 0     ; Initialize source index
MOV DI, 9     ; Initialize destination index (length of string - 1)
; String data
MOV BYTE PTR [SI], 'H'
MOV BYTE PTR [SI + 1], 'e'
MOV BYTE PTR [SI + 2], 'l'
MOV BYTE PTR [SI + 3], 'l'
MOV BYTE PTR [SI + 4], 'o'
MOV BYTE PTR [SI + 5], ' '
MOV BYTE PTR [SI + 6], 'W'
```

```
MOV BYTE PTR [SI + 7], 'o'
MOV BYTE PTR [SI + 8], 'r'
MOV BYTE PTR [SI + 9], 'l'
MOV BYTE PTR [SI + 10], 'd'
; Reverse the string
MOV CX, 5    ; Half the length of the string
REVERSE_LOOP:
MOV AL, [SI]  ; Load character from start
MOV BL, [SI + DI] ; Load character from end
MOV [SI + DI], AL ; Store start character at end
MOV [SI], BL  ; Store end character at start
INC SI        ; Move to next character from start
DEC DI        ; Move to next character from end
LOOP REVERSE_LOOP ; Repeat until middle of string
HLT           ; Halt the program
```

String Length Calculation

```
ORG 100h     ; Origin, start at address 100h
MOV SI, 0    ; Initialize source index
MOV CX, 0    ; Initialize counter for length
; String data (null-terminated)
MOV BYTE PTR [SI], 'H'
MOV BYTE PTR [SI + 1], 'e'
MOV BYTE PTR [SI + 2], 'l'
MOV BYTE PTR [SI + 3], 'l'
MOV BYTE PTR [SI + 4], 'o'
MOV BYTE PTR [SI + 5], 0   ; Null terminator
; Calculate string length
COUNT_LENGTH:
```

```
CMP BYTE PTR [SI], 0     ; Check for null terminator
JE END_COUNT            ; Jump if end of string
INC SI                  ; Move to next character
INC CX                  ; Increment length counter
JMP COUNT_LENGTH        ; Repeat until null terminator found
END_COUNT:
; CX now contains the length of the string excluding the null terminator
HLT        ; Halt the program
```

Palindrome Check for String

```
ORG 100h     ; Origin, start at address 100h
MOV SI, 0    ; Initialize source index
MOV DI, 0    ; Initialize destination index
; String data (null-terminated)
MOV BYTE PTR [SI], 'r'
MOV BYTE PTR [SI + 1], 'a'
MOV BYTE PTR [SI + 2], 'c'
MOV BYTE PTR [SI + 3], 'e'
MOV BYTE PTR [SI + 4], 'c'
MOV BYTE PTR [SI + 5], 'a'
MOV BYTE PTR [SI + 6], 'r'
MOV BYTE PTR [SI + 7], 0   ; Null terminator
; Calculate string length (excluding null terminator)
MOV CX, 0    ; Initialize counter for length
COUNT_LENGTH:
CMP BYTE PTR [SI + CX], 0  ; Check for null terminator
JE PALINDROME_CHECK       ; Jump if end of string
INC CX                    ; Increment length counter
JMP COUNT_LENGTH          ; Repeat until null terminator found
```

```asm
; Check palindrome
PALINDROME_CHECK:
DEC CX        ; Adjust length to actual characters
MOV BX, CX    ; BX = Length - 1
COMPARE_LOOP:
MOV AL, [SI + DI]     ; Load character from start
MOV DL, [SI + BX]     ; Load character from end
CMP AL, DL            ; Compare characters
JNE NOT_PALINDROME    ; Jump if not equal
INC DI               ; Move to next character from start
DEC BX               ; Move to previous character from end
CMP DI, CX           ; Compare indices
JBE COMPARE_LOOP     ; Repeat until middle of string
; String is palindrome
MOV DL, 'Y'   ; Load 'Y' for Yes
JMP END
; String is not palindrome
NOT_PALINDROME:
MOV DL, 'N'   ; Load 'N' for No
; End of program
END:
HLT           ; Halt the program
```

Fibonacci Series Generation

```asm
ORG 100h      ; Origin, start at address 100h
MOV CX, 10    ; Number of Fibonacci numbers to generate
MOV SI, 0     ; Initialize index
MOV BX, 0     ; Initialize F(0)
MOV AX, 1     ; Initialize F(1)
```

```asm
; Print initial two Fibonacci numbers
MOV DL, '0'
MOV AH, 2
INT 21h      ; Print character
MOV DL, ','
INT 21h      ; Print comma and space
MOV DL, '1'
INT 21h      ; Print character
; Generate Fibonacci series
FIB_LOOP:
ADD BX, AX   ; BX = F(n-1) + F(n-2)
MOV AX, BX   ; F(n-1) = F(n-2)
SUB CX, 1    ; Decrement count
JZ END_FIB   ; Jump if zero
MOV DL, ','  ; Print comma and space
INT 21h      ; Print character
MOV DL, ' '
INT 21h      ; Print space
ADD SI, 1    ; Increment index
JMP FIB_LOOP ; Repeat loop
END_FIB:
HLT          ; Halt the program
```

Factorial Calculation

```asm
ORG 100h     ; Origin, start at address 100h
MOV CX, 5    ; Calculate factorial of 5
MOV AX, 1    ; Initialize factorial to 1
FACTORIAL_LOOP:
MUL CX       ; Multiply AX by CX
```

LOOP FACTORIAL_LOOP ; Decrement CX and repeat loop until CX = 0

HLT   ; Halt the program

GCD of Two Numbers

ORG 100h   ; Origin, start at address 100h

MOV AX, 36   ; Load first number

MOV BX, 60   ; Load second number

GCD_LOOP:

CMP AX, BX   ; Compare AX and BX

JE GCD_FOUND   ; If equal, AX contains GCD

JB SWAP   ; If AX < BX, swap AX and BX

SUB AX, BX   ; Subtract BX from AX

JMP GCD_LOOP ; Repeat loop

SWAP:

XCHG AX, BX   ; Swap AX and BX

JMP GCD_LOOP ; Repeat loop

GCD_FOUND:

HLT   ; Halt the program

LCM of Two Numbers

ORG 100h   ; Origin, start at address 100h

MOV AX, 12   ; Load first number

MOV BX, 18   ; Load second number

; Calculate LCM using the formula LCM(a, b) = |a * b| / GCD(a, b)

MOV CX, AX   ; Save first number in CX

MOV DX, BX   ; Save second number in DX

; Calculate GCD of AX and BX

GCD_LOOP:

CMP AX, BX   ; Compare AX and BX

```
JE GCD_FOUND   ; If equal, AX contains GCD
JB SWAP        ; If AX < BX, swap AX and BX
SUB AX, BX     ; Subtract BX from AX
JMP GCD_LOOP   ; Repeat loop
SWAP:
XCHG AX, BX    ; Swap AX and BX
JMP GCD_LOOP   ; Repeat loop
GCD_FOUND:
; Calculate LCM
MUL DX         ; AX = AX * DX
XCHG CX, DX    ; Swap CX and DX
DIV CX         ; AX = AX / CX (GCD)
; AX now contains LCM
HLT            ; Halt the program
```

Prime Number Check

```
ORG 100h       ; Origin, start at address 100h
MOV AX, 11     ; Load number to check for prime
; Check for prime
MOV CX, 2      ; Start divisor from 2
CHECK_PRIME:
MOV DX, 0      ; Clear DX for DIV operation
DIV CX         ; AX / CX, quotient in AX, remainder in DX
CMP DX, 0      ; Check remainder
JE NOT_PRIME   ; If remainder is zero, number is not prime
INC CX         ; Increment divisor
CMP CX, AX     ; Compare divisor with number
JB CHECK_PRIME ; Loop if divisor is less than number
; Number is prime
```

```
MOV DL, 'Y'   ; Load 'Y' for Yes
JMP END
; Number is not prime
NOT_PRIME:
MOV DL, 'N'   ; Load 'N' for No
; End of program
END:
HLT          ; Halt the program
```

Prime Numbers in a Range

```
ORG 100h      ; Origin, start at address 100h
MOV CX, 10    ; Find prime numbers up to 10
; Print initial message
MOV DX, OFFSET MESSAGE
MOV AH, 9
INT 21h
MOV AX, 2     ; Start with 2 (first prime number)
FIND_PRIME:
MOV BX, 2     ; Divisor starts from 2
CHECK_PRIME:
MOV DX, 0     ; Clear DX for DIV operation
DIV BX        ; AX / BX, quotient in AX, remainder in DX
CMP DX, 0     ; Check remainder
JE NOT_PRIME  ; If remainder is zero, number is not prime
INC BX        ; Increment divisor
CMP BX, AX    ; Compare divisor with number
JB CHECK_PRIME ; Loop if divisor is less than number
; Print prime number
MOV AH, 2     ; Print function
```

```
MOV DL,''   ; Separator
INT 21h
MOV DX, AX    ; Print prime number
MOV AH, 2
INT 21h
; Check next number
INC AX        ; Increment number
CMP AX, CX    ; Compare number with range
JBE FIND_PRIME ; Loop if within range
HLT           ; Halt the program
```

Armstrong Number Check

```
ORG 100h      ; Origin, start at address 100h
MOV AX, 153   ; Load number to check for Armstrong
; Check Armstrong number
MOV BX, AX    ; Save original number
MOV CX, 0     ; Initialize sum of cubes of digits
CALC_SUM:
MOV DX, 0     ; Clear DX for DIV operation
MOV BX, AX    ; Restore original number
DIV TEN       ; Divide AX by 10, quotient in AX, remainder in DX
MUL DX        ; AX = DX * DX
ADD CX, AX    ; Add AX to CX
CMP AX, 0     ; Check if AX is zero
JNZ CALC_SUM  ; Loop if not zero
CMP CX, BX    ; Compare sum with original number
JE IS_ARMSTRONG ; If equal, number is Armstrong
; Number is not Armstrong
MOV DL, 'N'   ; Load 'N' for No
```

JMP END
; Number is Armstrong
IS_ARMSTRONG:
MOV DL, 'Y'   ; Load 'Y' for Yes
; End of program
END:
HLT   ; Halt the program
TEN DW 10   ; Constant 10 for division

Find Square of a Number

ORG 100h   ; Origin, start at address 100h
MOV AX, 8   ; Load number to calculate square
; Calculate square
MUL AX   ; AX = AX * AX
HLT   ; Halt the program

Find Cube of a Number

ORG 100h   ; Origin, start at address 100h
MOV AX, 5   ; Load number to calculate cube
; Calculate cube
MUL AX   ; AX = AX * AX (square)
MOV BX, AX   ; Save the square in BX
MUL BX   ; AX = AX * BX (cube)
HLT   ; Halt the program

Linear Search in Array

ORG 100h   ; Origin, start at address 100h
MOV SI, 0   ; Initialize source index
MOV CX, 5   ; Array size

```asm
MOV AL, 37h   ; Value to search for
MOV BL, 0FFh  ; Initialize result to not found (0FFh)
; Array data
MOV BYTE PTR [SI], 25h
MOV BYTE PTR [SI + 1], 37h
MOV BYTE PTR [SI + 2], 12h
MOV BYTE PTR [SI + 3], 45h
MOV BYTE PTR [SI + 4], 30h
; Perform linear search
SEARCH_LOOP:
CMP AL, [SI]  ; Compare AL with array element
JE FOUND      ; If equal, value is found
INC SI        ; Move to the next element
LOOP SEARCH_LOOP ; Repeat for all elements
JMP NOT_FOUND ; If loop completes, value is not found
FOUND:
MOV BL, SI    ; Store the index where value is found
NOT_FOUND:
HLT           ; Halt the program
```

Binary Search in Array

```asm
ORG 100h      ; Origin, start at address 100h
MOV AX, 0     ; Initialize start index
MOV CX, 4     ; Initialize end index
MOV DL, 37h   ; Value to search for
MOV BL, 0FFh  ; Initialize result to not found (0FFh)
; Sorted array data
MOV BYTE PTR [100h], 12h
MOV BYTE PTR [101h], 25h
```

```
MOV BYTE PTR [102h], 37h
MOV BYTE PTR [103h], 45h
MOV BYTE PTR [104h], 50h
BINARY_SEARCH:
CMP AX, CX    ; Compare start and end indices
JG NOT_FOUND  ; If start > end, value is not found
MOV BX, AX    ; Calculate mid index
ADD BX, CX
SHR BX, 1
MOV SI, 100h  ; Array base address
MOV AL, [SI + BX] ; Load middle element
CMP DL, AL    ; Compare value with middle element
JE FOUND      ; If equal, value is found
JL SEARCH_LEFT ; If less, search left half
; Search right half
MOV AX, BX
INC AX
JMP BINARY_SEARCH
SEARCH_LEFT:
MOV CX, BX
DEC CX
JMP BINARY_SEARCH
FOUND:
MOV BL, BX    ; Store the index where value is found
NOT_FOUND:
HLT           ; Halt the program
```

Matrix Addition

```
ORG 100h      ; Origin, start at address 100h
```

```
; Matrix A
MOV BYTE PTR [200h], 1
MOV BYTE PTR [201h], 2
MOV BYTE PTR [202h], 3
MOV BYTE PTR [203h], 4
; Matrix B
MOV BYTE PTR [204h], 5
MOV BYTE PTR [205h], 6
MOV BYTE PTR [206h], 7
MOV BYTE PTR [207h], 8
; Result Matrix C at 208h
; Add matrices
MOV SI, 200h   ; Base address of Matrix A
MOV DI, 204h   ; Base address of Matrix B
MOV BX, 208h   ; Base address of Result Matrix C
MOV CX, 4      ; Number of elements in matrices
ADD_LOOP:
MOV AL, [SI]   ; Load element from Matrix A
ADD AL, [DI]   ; Add element from Matrix B
MOV [BX], AL   ; Store result in Matrix C
INC SI         ; Move to the next element in Matrix A
INC DI         ; Move to the next element in Matrix B
INC BX         ; Move to the next element in Matrix C
LOOP ADD_LOOP  ; Repeat for all elements
HLT            ; Halt the program
```

Find Cube of a Number

```
ORG 100h     ; Origin, start at address 100h
MOV AX, 5    ; Load number to calculate cube
```

```
; Calculate cube
MUL AX      ; AX = AX * AX (square)
MOV BX, AX   ; Save the square in BX
MUL BX      ; AX = AX * BX (cube)
HLT         ; Halt the program
```

Linear Search in Array

```
ORG 100h     ; Origin, start at address 100h
MOV SI, 0    ; Initialize source index
MOV CX, 5    ; Array size
MOV AL, 37h  ; Value to search for
MOV BL, 0FFh ; Initialize result to not found (0FFh)
; Array data
MOV BYTE PTR [SI], 25h
MOV BYTE PTR [SI + 1], 37h
MOV BYTE PTR [SI + 2], 12h
MOV BYTE PTR [SI + 3], 45h
MOV BYTE PTR [SI + 4], 30h
; Perform linear search
SEARCH_LOOP:
CMP AL, [SI] ; Compare AL with array element
JE FOUND     ; If equal, value is found
INC SI       ; Move to the next element
LOOP SEARCH_LOOP ; Repeat for all elements
JMP NOT_FOUND ; If loop completes, value is not found
FOUND:
MOV BL, SI   ; Store the index where value is found
NOT_FOUND:
HLT          ; Halt the program
```

Binary Search in Array

```
ORG 100h      ; Origin, start at address 100h
MOV AX, 0     ; Initialize start index
MOV CX, 4     ; Initialize end index
MOV DL, 37h   ; Value to search for
MOV BL, 0FFh  ; Initialize result to not found (0FFh)
; Sorted array data
MOV BYTE PTR [100h], 12h
MOV BYTE PTR [101h], 25h
MOV BYTE PTR [102h], 37h
MOV BYTE PTR [103h], 45h
MOV BYTE PTR [104h], 50h
BINARY_SEARCH:
CMP AX, CX    ; Compare start and end indices
JG NOT_FOUND  ; If start > end, value is not found
MOV BX, AX    ; Calculate mid index
ADD BX, CX
SHR BX, 1
MOV SI, 100h  ; Array base address
MOV AL, [SI + BX] ; Load middle element
CMP DL, AL    ; Compare value with middle element
JE FOUND      ; If equal, value is found
JL SEARCH_LEFT ; If less, search left half
; Search right half
MOV AX, BX
INC AX
JMP BINARY_SEARCH
SEARCH_LEFT:
MOV CX, BX
```

DEC CX

JMP BINARY_SEARCH

FOUND:

MOV BL, BX   ; Store the index where value is found

NOT_FOUND:

HLT   ; Halt the program

Matrix Addition

ORG 100h   ; Origin, start at address 100h

; Matrix A

MOV BYTE PTR [200h], 1

MOV BYTE PTR [201h], 2

MOV BYTE PTR [202h], 3

MOV BYTE PTR [203h], 4

; Matrix B

MOV BYTE PTR [204h], 5

MOV BYTE PTR [205h], 6

MOV BYTE PTR [206h], 7

MOV BYTE PTR [207h], 8

; Result Matrix C at 208h

; Add matrices

MOV SI, 200h   ; Base address of Matrix A

MOV DI, 204h   ; Base address of Matrix B

MOV BX, 208h   ; Base address of Result Matrix C

MOV CX, 4   ; Number of elements in matrices

ADD_LOOP:

MOV AL, [SI]   ; Load element from Matrix A

ADD AL, [DI]   ; Add element from Matrix B

MOV [BX], AL   ; Store result in Matrix C

```
INC SI        ; Move to the next element in Matrix A
INC DI        ; Move to the next element in Matrix B
INC BX        ; Move to the next element in Matrix C
LOOP ADD_LOOP ; Repeat for all elements
HLT           ; Halt the program
```

Sum of Diagonals of a Matrix

```
ORG 100h     ; Origin, start at address 100h
; Matrix A
MOV BYTE PTR [200h], 1
MOV BYTE PTR [201h], 2
MOV BYTE PTR [202h], 3
MOV BYTE PTR [203h], 4
; Calculate sum of diagonals
MOV SI, 200h   ; Base address of Matrix A
MOV AL, [SI]   ; Load A[0][0]
ADD AL, [SI + 3] ; Add A[1][1]
MOV BL, [SI + 1] ; Load A[0][1]
ADD BL, [SI + 2] ; Add A[1][0]
; AL contains sum of main diagonal
; BL contains sum of off diagonal
HLT           ; Halt the program
```

Sum of Rows of a Matrix

```
ORG 100h     ; Origin, start at address 100h
; Matrix A
MOV BYTE PTR [200h], 1
MOV BYTE PTR [201h], 2
MOV BYTE PTR [202h], 3
```

MOV BYTE PTR [203h], 4

; Calculate sum of rows

MOV SI, 200h   ; Base address of Matrix A

MOV AL, [SI]   ; Load A[0][0]

ADD AL, [SI + 1] ; Add A[0][1]

MOV [204h], AL ; Store sum of first row

MOV AL, [SI + 2] ; Load A[1][0]

ADD AL, [SI + 3] ; Add A[1][1]

MOV [205h], AL ; Store sum of second row

HLT   ; Halt the program

Sum of Columns of a Matrix

ORG 100h   ; Origin, start at address 100h

; Matrix A

MOV BYTE PTR [200h], 1

MOV BYTE PTR [201h], 2

MOV BYTE PTR [202h], 3

MOV BYTE PTR [203h], 4

; Calculate sum of columns

MOV SI, 200h   ; Base address of Matrix A

MOV AL, [SI]   ; Load A[0][0]

ADD AL, [SI + 2] ; Add A[1][0]

MOV [204h], AL ; Store sum of first column

MOV AL, [SI + 1] ; Load A[0][1]

ADD AL, [SI + 3] ; Add A[1][1]

MOV [205h], AL ; Store sum of second column

HLT   ; Halt the program

Bitwise AND Operation

```
ORG 100h     ; Origin, start at address 100h
MOV AL, 55h  ; Load first number into AL
MOV BL, AAh  ; Load second number into BL
AND AL, BL   ; Perform bitwise AND operation, result in AL
HLT          ; Halt the program
```

Bitwise OR Operation

```
ORG 100h     ; Origin, start at address 100h
MOV AL, 55h  ; Load first number into AL
MOV BL, AAh  ; Load second number into BL
OR AL, BL    ; Perform bitwise OR operation, result in AL
HLT          ; Halt the program
```

Bitwise XOR Operation

```
ORG 100h     ; Origin, start at address 100h
MOV AL, 55h  ; Load first number into AL
MOV BL, AAh  ; Load second number into BL
XOR AL, BL   ; Perform bitwise XOR operation, result in AL
HLT          ; Halt the program
```

Bitwise NOT Operation

```
ORG 100h     ; Origin, start at address 100h
MOV AL, 55h  ; Load number into AL
NOT AL       ; Perform bitwise NOT operation, result in AL
HLT          ; Halt the program
```

Left Rotate a Byte

```
ORG 100h     ; Origin, start at address 100h
MOV AL, 96h  ; Load the byte into AL
ROL AL, 1    ; Rotate AL left by 1 bit
HLT          ; Halt the program
```

Right Rotate a Byte

```
ORG 100h     ; Origin, start at address 100h
MOV AL, 96h  ; Load the byte into AL
ROR AL, 1    ; Rotate AL right by 1 bit
HLT          ; Halt the program
```

Left Shift a Byte

```
ORG 100h     ; Origin, start at address 100h
MOV AL, 96h  ; Load the byte into AL
SHL AL, 1    ; Shift AL left by 1 bit
HLT          ; Halt the program
```

Right Shift a Byte

```
ORG 100h     ; Origin, start at address 100h
MOV AL, 96h  ; Load the byte into AL
SHR AL, 1    ; Shift AL right by 1 bit
HLT          ; Halt the program
```

Swap Two Numbers

```
ORG 100h     ; Origin, start at address 100h
MOV AL, 5Ah  ; Load first number into AL
MOV BL, 3Ch  ; Load second number into BL
XCHG AL, BL  ; Swap the values of AL and BL
```

```
HLT          ; Halt the program
```

Interchange First and Last Digits of a Number

```
ORG 100h     ; Origin, start at address 100h
MOV AX, 1234h ; Load the number into AX
; Extract last digit
MOV BX, AX   ; Copy AX to BX
MOV CX, 10   ; Set divisor to 10
MOV DX, 0    ; Clear DX
DIV CX       ; Divide AX by 10, quotient in AX, remainder in DX (last digit)
MOV DL, AH   ; Store last digit in DL
MOV AL, 0    ; Clear AL
MOV AH, BL   ; Move last digit to AH
XCHG AH, DL  ; Swap first and last digits
MOV BL, 0    ; Clear BL
MOV BH, 0    ; Clear BH
; Construct the new number
MOV BX, 1000h ; Set BX to 1000 (assuming 4-digit number)
MUL BX       ; Multiply DL by 1000
ADD AX, BX   ; Add original middle digits to AX
HLT          ; Halt the program
```

Calculate Simple Interest

```
ORG 100h     ; Origin, start at address 100h
MOV AX, 1000  ; Principal amount (P)
MOV BX, 5    ; Rate of interest (R)
MOV CX, 2    ; Time period in years (T)
; Calculate simple interest (SI = P * R * T / 100)
MUL BX       ; AX = P * R
```

```
MUL CX      ; AX = (P * R) * T
MOV BX, 100  ; Set BX to 100
DIV BX      ; AX = (P * R * T) / 100
HLT         ; Halt the program
```

Calculate Compound Interest

```
ORG 100h     ; Origin, start at address 100h
MOV AX, 1000  ; Principal amount (P)
MOV BX, 5    ; Rate of interest (R) in percentage
MOV CX, 2    ; Time period in years (T)
; Calculate compound interest (A = P * (1 + R/100)^T)
MOV DX, 100   ; Set DX to 100
MOV SI, BX   ; Copy R to SI
DIV DX       ; Divide BX by 100 to get R/100 in AX
ADD AX, 1    ; 1 + R/100
MOV SI, AX   ; Copy (1 + R/100) to SI
MOV AX, 1000  ; Reload principal amount to AX
COMPOUND_LOOP:
MUL SI       ; AX = AX * (1 + R/100)
DEC CX       ; Decrease time period
JNZ COMPOUND_LOOP ; Repeat for T times
; AX now contains the compound amount (A)
SUB AX, 1000  ; To get the compound interest (A - P)
HLT         ; Halt the program
```

Find ASCII Value of a Character

```
ORG 100h     ; Origin, start at address 100h
MOV AL, 'A'  ; Load character into AL
; The ASCII value of the character is already in AL
```

```
MOV BL, AL   ; Move ASCII value to BL for demonstration
HLT          ; Halt the program
```

Character to Uppercase Conversion

```
ORG 100h      ; Origin, start at address 100h
MOV AL, 'b'   ; Load lowercase character into AL
; Check if the character is lowercase
CMP AL, 'a'   ; Compare with 'a'
JL NOT_LOWER  ; If less, it's not a lowercase letter
CMP AL, 'z'   ; Compare with 'z'
JG NOT_LOWER  ; If greater, it's not a lowercase letter
; Convert to uppercase
SUB AL, 20h   ; Subtract 32 to convert to uppercase
NOT_LOWER:
MOV BL, AL    ; Move the result to BL for demonstration
HLT           ; Halt the program
```

Character to Lowercase Conversion

```
ORG 100h      ; Origin, start at address 100h
MOV AL, 'B'   ; Load uppercase character into AL
; Check if the character is uppercase
CMP AL, 'A'   ; Compare with 'A'
JL NOT_UPPER  ; If less, it's not an uppercase letter
CMP AL, 'Z'   ; Compare with 'Z'
JG NOT_UPPER  ; If greater, it's not an uppercase letter
; Convert to lowercase
ADD AL, 20h   ; Add 32 to convert to lowercase
NOT_UPPER:
MOV BL, AL    ; Move the result to BL for demonstration
```

```
HLT        ; Halt the program
```

Find Power of a Number

```
ORG 100h     ; Origin, start at address 100h
MOV AX, 2    ; Base
MOV CX, 3    ; Exponent
MOV BX, AX   ; Copy base to BX
DEC CX       ; Decrease exponent by 1
POWER_LOOP:
MUL BX       ; Multiply AX by base
DEC CX       ; Decrease exponent
JNZ POWER_LOOP ; Repeat until exponent is zero
HLT          ; Halt the program
```

Find Square Root of a Number

```
ORG 100h     ; Origin, start at address 100h
MOV AX, 36   ; Number to find the square root of
MOV BX, 1    ; Initial guess
MOV CX, 10   ; Number of iterations
SQRT_LOOP:
MOV DX, 0    ; Clear DX for DIV
DIV BX       ; Divide AX by BX, quotient in AX
ADD AX, BX   ; AX = (AX + BX)
SHR AX, 1    ; AX = AX / 2
MOV BX, AX   ; Update guess
LOOP SQRT_LOOP ; Repeat for the specified iterations
HLT          ; Halt the program
```

Decimal to Binary Conversion

```
ORG 100h     ; Origin, start at address 100h
MOV AX, 10   ; Load decimal number
MOV CX, 16   ; Number of bits
MOV BX, 0    ; Clear BX to store binary result
CONVERT_LOOP:
SHL BX, 1    ; Shift left BX by 1 bit
MOV DX, 0    ; Clear DX for DIV
DIV WORD PTR [TEN] ; Divide AX by 10
ADD BL, AL   ; Add remainder to BL
LOOP CONVERT_LOOP ; Repeat for all bits
HLT          ; Halt the program
TEN DW 10    ; Define constant 10
```

Binary to Decimal Conversion

```
ORG 100h     ; Origin, start at address 100h
MOV AX, 1011b ; Load binary number (example: 11 in decimal)
MOV CX, 10   ; Multiplier for decimal conversion
MOV BX, 0    ; Clear BX to store decimal result
CONVERT_LOOP:
SHR AX, 1    ; Shift right AX by 1 bit
JNC NO_ADD   ; If no carry, skip addition
ADD BX, CX   ; Add multiplier to BX
NO_ADD:
ADD CX, CX   ; Double the multiplier
CMP AX, 0    ; Check if AX is zero
JNZ CONVERT_LOOP ; Repeat until AX is zero
HLT          ; Halt the program
```

Decimal to Hexadecimal Conversion

```
ORG 100h      ; Origin, start at address 100h
MOV AX, 1234  ; Load decimal number
MOV CX, 0     ; Clear CX to store hexadecimal result
MOV BX, 10h   ; Set base to 16
CONVERT_LOOP:
XOR DX, DX    ; Clear DX for DIV
DIV BX        ; Divide AX by 16, quotient in AX, remainder in DX
ADD DL, 30h   ; Convert remainder to ASCII
CMP DL, 39h   ; If remainder > 9
JLE STORE_DIGIT
ADD DL, 7h    ; Adjust ASCII for A-F
STORE_DIGIT:
PUSH DX       ; Push remainder onto stack
INC CX        ; Increment digit counter
CMP AX, 0     ; Check if quotient is zero
JNZ CONVERT_LOOP ; Repeat until quotient is zero
; Output hexadecimal result
MOV AH, 2     ; Set up for output
POP_LOOP:
POP DX        ; Pop digit from stack
MOV DL, DH    ; Move digit to DL for output
INT 21h       ; Output character
LOOP POP_LOOP ; Repeat for all digits
HLT           ; Halt the program
```

Hexadecimal to Decimal Conversion

```
ORG 100h      ; Origin, start at address 100h
MOV SI, HEX_STRING ; Load address of hexadecimal string
```

```asm
MOV BX, 10h  ; Set base to 16
MOV CX, 0    ; Clear CX to store result
CONVERT_LOOP:
MOV AL, [SI] ; Load character from string
CMP AL, 0    ; Check for end of string
JE DONE
; Convert ASCII to numeric value
SUB AL, '0'
CMP AL, 9
JLE CONTINUE
SUB AL, 7h   ; Adjust for A-F
CONTINUE:
MUL BX       ; Multiply CX by 16
ADD CX, AX   ; Add numeric value to CX
INC SI       ; Move to next character
JMP CONVERT_LOOP
DONE:
MOV AX, CX   ; Move result to AX
HLT          ; Halt the program
HEX_STRING DB '4D2', 0  ; Example hexadecimal string '4D2' (1234 in decimal)
```

Decimal to Octal Conversion

```asm
ORG 100h     ; Origin, start at address 100h
MOV AX, 1234 ; Load decimal number
MOV CX, 0    ; Clear CX to store octal result
MOV BX, 8    ; Set base to 8
CONVERT_LOOP:
XOR DX, DX   ; Clear DX for DIV
DIV BX       ; Divide AX by 8, quotient in AX, remainder in DX
```

```
ADD DL, 30h   ; Convert remainder to ASCII
PUSH DX       ; Push remainder onto stack
INC CX        ; Increment digit counter
CMP AX, 0     ; Check if quotient is zero
JNZ CONVERT_LOOP ; Repeat until quotient is zero
; Output octal result
MOV AH, 2     ; Set up for output
POP_LOOP:
POP DX        ; Pop digit from stack
MOV DL, DH    ; Move digit to DL for output
INT 21h       ; Output character
LOOP POP_LOOP ; Repeat for all digits
HLT           ; Halt the program
```

Octal to Decimal Conversion

```
ORG 100h      ; Origin, start at address 100h
MOV SI, OCT_STRING ; Load address of octal string
MOV BX, 8     ; Set base to 8
MOV CX, 0     ; Clear CX to store result
CONVERT_LOOP:
MOV AL, [SI]  ; Load character from string
CMP AL, 0     ; Check for end of string
JE DONE
; Convert ASCII to numeric value
SUB AL, '0'
MUL BX        ; Multiply CX by 8
ADD CX, AX    ; Add numeric value to CX
INC SI        ; Move to next character
JMP CONVERT_LOOP
```

```
DONE:
MOV AX, CX    ; Move result to AX
HLT           ; Halt the program
```

Hexadecimal to Binary Conversion

```
ORG 100h      ; Origin, start at address 100h
MOV SI, HEX_STRING ; Load address of hexadecimal string
MOV DI, BINARY_RESULT ; Load address for binary result
CONVERT_LOOP:
MOV AL, [SI]  ; Load character from string
CMP AL, 0     ; Check for end of string
JE DONE
; Convert ASCII to numeric value
SUB AL, '0'
CMP AL, 9
JLE CONTINUE
SUB AL, 7h    ; Adjust for A-F
CONTINUE:
MOV BL, 4     ; Set bit position counter
TO_BINARY:
MOV AH, AL
AND AH, 0Fh   ; Mask lower nibble
MOV CL, BL
SHR AH, CL
AND AH, 1
ADD AH, 30h   ; Convert bit to ASCII
MOV [DI], AH  ; Store result
INC DI        ; Move to next position
DEC BL
```

```
JNZ TO_BINARY
INC SI        ; Move to next character
JMP CONVERT_LOOP
DONE:
MOV BYTE PTR [DI], 0 ; Null terminate the binary result
HLT           ; Halt the program
HEX_STRING DB 'A3', 0 ; Example hexadecimal string 'A3'
BINARY_RESULT DB 16 DUP(?) ; Space for binary result
```

Binary to Hexadecimal Conversion

```
ORG 100h      ; Origin, start at address 100h
MOV SI, BINARY_STRING ; Load address of binary string
MOV DI, HEX_RESULT    ; Load address for hexadecimal result
CONVERT_LOOP:
MOV CX, 4     ; Set bit counter to 4
XOR BL, BL    ; Clear BL to build a nibble
BUILD_NIBBLE:
MOV AL, [SI]  ; Load bit character
CMP AL, 0     ; Check for end of string
JE DONE
SUB AL, 30h   ; Convert ASCII to bit
SHL BL, 1     ; Shift BL left to make room
OR BL, AL     ; Add bit to BL
INC SI        ; Move to next bit
DEC CX        ; Decrement bit counter
JNZ BUILD_NIBBLE
; Convert nibble to hexadecimal ASCII
ADD BL, 30h   ; Convert to ASCII
CMP BL, 39h   ; Check if greater than '9'
```

```
JLE STORE_RESULT
ADD BL, 7h    ; Adjust for A-F
STORE_RESULT:
MOV [DI], BL  ; Store hexadecimal character
INC DI        ; Move to next position
JMP CONVERT_LOOP
DONE:
MOV BYTE PTR [DI], 0 ; Null terminate the hexadecimal result
HLT           ; Halt the program
BINARY_STRING DB '10100011', 0 ; Example binary string '10100011'
HEX_RESULT DB 4 DUP(?) ; Space for hexadecimal result
```

Hexadecimal to ASCII Conversion

```
ORG 100h      ; Origin, start at address 100h
MOV AX, '41'  ; Load hexadecimal value ('41' for 'A')
; Convert high nibble
MOV AH, AL
SHR AH, 4
ADD AH, 30h
CMP AH, 39h
JLE STORE_HIGH
ADD AH, 7h
STORE_HIGH:
MOV BL, AH    ; Store high nibble ASCII
; Convert low nibble
MOV AH, AL
AND AH, 0Fh
ADD AH, 30h
CMP AH, 39h
```

```
JLE STORE_LOW
ADD AH, 7h
STORE_LOW:
MOV BH, AH    ; Store low nibble ASCII
HLT           ; Halt the program
```

ASCII to Hexadecimal Conversion

```
ORG 100h     ; Origin, start at address 100h
MOV AL, 'A'  ; Load ASCII character into AL
; Convert ASCII to hexadecimal
MOV BL, AL
SUB BL, 30h
CMP BL, 9
JLE CONVERT
SUB BL, 7h
CONVERT:
MOV BH, BL    ; Store hexadecimal result in BH
HLT           ; Halt the program
```

Display Character String

```
ORG 100h      ; Origin, start at address 100h
MOV DX, OFFSET MESSAGE ; Load address of message string
MOV AH, 09h   ; DOS function to display string
INT 21h       ; Call DOS interrupt
HLT           ; Halt the program
MESSAGE DB 'Hello, World!', '$' ; Null-terminated string with '$' as end marker
```

Display ASCII Table

```
ORG 100h      ; Origin, start at address 100h
```

```asm
MOV CX, 128  ; Number of ASCII characters to display
MOV AL, 0    ; Start with ASCII 0
DISPLAY_LOOP:
MOV AH, 2    ; DOS function to display character
INT 21h      ; Call DOS interrupt
MOV AH, 2    ; DOS function to display space
MOV DL, ' '
INT 21h      ; Call DOS interrupt
INC AL       ; Move to the next ASCII character
LOOP DISPLAY_LOOP ; Repeat for all characters
HLT          ; Halt the program
```

Find Sum of Digits of a Number

```asm
ORG 100h     ; Origin, start at address 100h
MOV AX, 1234 ; Load the number into AX
MOV CX, 0    ; Initialize sum to 0
SUM_LOOP:
MOV DX, 0    ; Clear DX for DIV
MOV BX, 10   ; Set divisor to 10
DIV BX       ; Divide AX by 10, quotient in AX, remainder in DX
ADD CX, DX   ; Add remainder (digit) to sum
CMP AX, 0    ; Check if quotient is zero
JNZ SUM_LOOP ; Repeat until quotient is zero
; CX now contains the sum of the digits
HLT          ; Halt the program
```

Reverse Digits of a Number

```asm
ORG 100h     ; Origin, start at address 100h
MOV AX, 1234 ; Load the number into AX
```

```
MOV BX, 0     ; Initialize reversed number to 0
REVERSE_LOOP:
MOV DX, 0     ; Clear DX for DIV
MOV CX, 10    ; Set divisor to 10
DIV CX        ; Divide AX by 10, quotient in AX, remainder in DX
ADD BX, DX    ; Add remainder (digit) to BX
CMP AX, 0     ; Check if quotient is zero
JZ DONE
MUL CX        ; Multiply BX by 10 to shift left
JMP REVERSE_LOOP ; Repeat until quotient is zero
DONE:
; BX now contains the reversed number
HLT           ; Halt the program
```

Check for Armstrong Number in a Range

```
ORG 100h      ; Origin, start at address 100h
MOV CX, 1     ; Start number
MOV BX, 999   ; End number
CHECK_LOOP:
MOV AX, CX    ; Copy number to AX
MOV DX, 0     ; Clear DX
MOV SI, AX    ; Copy number to SI for comparison
; Calculate sum of cubes of digits
SUM_OF_CUBES:
MOV BX, 10    ; Set divisor to 10
DIV BX        ; Divide AX by 10, quotient in AX, remainder in DX
MOV DI, DX    ; Move remainder to DI
MUL DI        ; Multiply remainder by itself
MUL DI        ; Multiply again to get cube
```

```
ADD SI, AX    ; Add cube to SI
CMP AX, 0     ; Check if quotient is zero
JNZ SUM_OF_CUBES ; Repeat until quotient is zero
CMP SI, CX    ; Compare sum of cubes to original number
JE ARMSTRONG  ; If equal, it is an Armstrong number
; Move to next number
INC CX
CMP CX, BX    ; Check if reached end of range
JLE CHECK_LOOP ; Repeat for all numbers in range
HLT           ; Halt the program
ARMSTRONG:
; Handle Armstrong number (e.g., print it or set a flag)
INC CX
CMP CX, BX    ; Check if reached end of range
JLE CHECK_LOOP ; Repeat for all numbers in range
HLT           ; Halt the program
```

Check for Perfect Number

```
ORG 100h      ; Origin, start at address 100h
MOV AX, 28    ; Load the number into AX (example: 28)
MOV BX, AX    ; Copy number to BX
MOV CX, 1     ; Initialize divisor to 1
MOV DX, 0     ; Initialize sum of divisors to 0
CHECK_DIVISORS:
MOV SI, BX    ; Copy number to SI for division
MOV DX, 0     ; Clear DX for DIV
DIV CX        ; Divide BX by CX, quotient in AX, remainder in DX
CMP DX, 0     ; Check if remainder is zero
JNE NOT_DIVISOR
```

ADD DX, CX   ; Add divisor to sum of divisors
NOT_DIVISOR:
INC CX   ; Move to next divisor
CMP CX, BX   ; Check if reached number
JLE CHECK_DIVISORS ; Repeat for all potential divisors
CMP DX, BX   ; Compare sum of divisors to original number
JE PERFECT   ; If equal, it is a perfect number
; Handle not perfect number (e.g., set a flag or print a message)
JMP DONE
PERFECT:
; Handle perfect number (e.g., set a flag or print a message)
DONE:
HLT   ; Halt the program

Find Sum of N Natural Numbers

ORG 100h   ; Origin, start at address 100h
MOV CX, 10   ; N (the number of natural numbers to sum)
MOV AX, 0   ; Initialize sum to 0
SUM_LOOP:
ADD AX, CX   ; Add CX to AX (sum)
DEC CX   ; Decrement CX
JNZ SUM_LOOP ; Repeat until CX is zero
; AX now contains the sum of the first N natural numbers
HLT   ; Halt the program

Find Sum of Squares of N Natural Numbers

ORG 100h   ; Origin, start at address 100h
MOV CX, 10   ; N (the number of natural numbers to sum the squares)
MOV AX, 0   ; Initialize sum to 0

```
SUM_SQUARES_LOOP:
MOV BX, CX    ; Copy CX to BX
MUL BX        ; AX = BX * BX (square of the number)
ADD DX, AX    ; Add AX to DX (sum of squares)
DEC CX        ; Decrement CX
JNZ SUM_SQUARES_LOOP ; Repeat until CX is zero
; DX now contains the sum of the squares of the first N natural numbers
HLT           ; Halt the program
```

Find Sum of Cubes of N Natural Numbers

```
ORG 100h      ; Origin, start at address 100h
MOV CX, 10    ; N (the number of natural numbers to sum the cubes)
MOV AX, 0     ; Initialize sum to 0
SUM_CUBES_LOOP:
MOV BX, CX    ; Copy CX to BX
MUL BX        ; AX = BX * BX (square of the number)
MUL BX        ; AX = AX * BX (cube of the number)
ADD DX, AX    ; Add AX to DX (sum of cubes)
DEC CX        ; Decrement CX
JNZ SUM_CUBES_LOOP ; Repeat until CX is zero
; DX now contains the sum of the cubes of the first N natural numbers
HLT           ; Halt the program
```

Generate Pascal's Triangle

```
ORG 100h      ; Origin, start at address 100h
MOV CX, 5     ; Number of rows in Pascal's Triangle
MOV SI, 200h  ; Start address for storing the triangle
PASCAL_LOOP:
MOV BX, CX    ; Copy row number to BX
```

```
MOV DX, 1     ; Initialize DX to 1 (first element in row)
STORE_ROW:
MOV [SI], DX  ; Store DX at address SI
ADD SI, 2     ; Move to next position in memory
MOV AX, DX    ; Copy DX to AX
MUL BX        ; AX = AX * BX (calculate next element)
MOV BX, CX    ; Copy row number to BX
DIV BX        ; Divide AX by BX to get next element
DEC BX        ; Decrement row counter
JNZ STORE_ROW ; Repeat until row counter is zero
DEC CX        ; Decrement number of rows
JNZ PASCAL_LOOP ; Repeat until all rows are generated
HLT           ; Halt the program
```

Count Vowels in a String

```
ORG 100h     ; Origin, start at address 100h
MOV SI, 200h ; Start address of the string
MOV CX, 0    ; Initialize vowel count to 0
; String data (null-terminated)
MOV BYTE PTR [SI], 'H'
MOV BYTE PTR [SI + 1], 'e'
MOV BYTE PTR [SI + 2], 'l'
MOV BYTE PTR [SI + 3], 'l'
MOV BYTE PTR [SI + 4], 'o'
MOV BYTE PTR [SI + 5], 0   ; Null terminator
COUNT_VOWELS:
MOV AL, [SI] ; Load character from string
CMP AL, 0    ; Check for null terminator
JE DONE
```

```
; Check if character is a vowel
CMP AL, 'A'
JE IS_VOWEL
CMP AL, 'E'
JE IS_VOWEL
CMP AL, 'I'
JE IS_VOWEL
CMP AL, 'O'
JE IS_VOWEL
CMP AL, 'U'
JE IS_VOWEL
CMP AL, 'a'
JE IS_VOWEL
CMP AL, 'e'
JE IS_VOWEL
CMP AL, 'i'
JE IS_VOWEL
CMP AL, 'o'
JE IS_VOWEL
CMP AL, 'u'
JE IS_VOWEL
JMP NOT_VOWEL
IS_VOWEL:
INC CX      ; Increment vowel count
NOT_VOWEL:
INC SI      ; Move to next character
JMP COUNT_VOWELS
DONE:
; CX now contains the number of vowels in the string
```

```
HLT         ; Halt the program
```

Count Consonants in a String

```
ORG 100h     ; Origin, start at address 100h
MOV SI, 200h  ; Start address of the string
MOV CX, 0    ; Initialize consonant count to 0
; String data (null-terminated)
MOV BYTE PTR [SI], 'H'
MOV BYTE PTR [SI + 1], 'e'
MOV BYTE PTR [SI + 2], 'l'
MOV BYTE PTR [SI + 3], 'l'
MOV BYTE PTR [SI + 4], 'o'
MOV BYTE PTR [SI + 5], 0   ; Null terminator
COUNT_CONSONANTS:
MOV AL, [SI]  ; Load character from string
CMP AL, 0    ; Check for null terminator
JE DONE
; Check if character is a consonant
CMP AL, 'A'
JE NOT_CONSONANT
CMP AL, 'E'
JE NOT_CONSONANT
CMP AL, 'I'
JE NOT_CONSONANT
CMP AL, 'O'
JE NOT_CONSONANT
CMP AL, 'U'
JE NOT_CONSONANT
CMP AL, 'a'
```

```asm
JE NOT_CONSONANT
CMP AL, 'e'
JE NOT_CONSONANT
CMP AL, 'i'
JE NOT_CONSONANT
CMP AL, 'o'
JE NOT_CONSONANT
CMP AL, 'u'
JE NOT_CONSONANT
CMP AL, 'A'
JB NOT_CONSONANT
CMP AL, 'Z'
JA NOT_CONSONANT
CMP AL, 'a'
JB NOT_CONSONANT
CMP AL, 'z'
JA NOT_CONSONANT
INC CX       ; Increment consonant count
NOT_CONSONANT:
INC SI       ; Move to next character
JMP COUNT_CONSONANTS
DONE:
; CX now contains the number of consonants in the string
HLT          ; Halt the program
```

Reverse Words in a Sentence

```asm
ORG 100h     ; Origin, start at address 100h
MOV SI, 200h  ; Start address of the string
MOV DI, 300h  ; Start address of the reversed string
```

```asm
MOV CX, 0    ; Initialize word length
; String data (null-terminated)
MOV BYTE PTR [SI], 'H'
MOV BYTE PTR [SI + 1], 'e'
MOV BYTE PTR [SI + 2], 'l'
MOV BYTE PTR [SI + 3], 'l'
MOV BYTE PTR [SI + 4], 'o'
MOV BYTE PTR [SI + 5], ' '
MOV BYTE PTR [SI + 6], 'W'
MOV BYTE PTR [SI + 7], 'o'
MOV BYTE PTR [SI + 8], 'r'
MOV BYTE PTR [SI + 9], 'l'
MOV BYTE PTR [SI + 10], 'd'
MOV BYTE PTR [SI + 11], 0   ; Null terminator
FIND_WORD_END:
MOV AL, [SI]
CMP AL, 0    ; Check for null terminator
JE REVERSE_LAST_WORD
CMP AL, ' '  ; Check for space
JE REVERSE_WORD
INC CX       ; Increment word length
INC SI       ; Move to next character
JMP FIND_WORD_END
REVERSE_WORD:
MOV BX, CX   ; Store word length in BX
SUB SI, CX   ; Move SI back to start of word
REVERSE_LOOP:
MOV AL, [SI]
MOV [DI], AL
```

```
INC SI
DEC CX
INC DI
CMP CX, 0
JNE REVERSE_LOOP
MOV AL, ' '
MOV [DI], AL ; Store space
INC DI
INC SI
MOV CX, BX
SUB CX, CX   ; Reset word length
JMP FIND_WORD_END
REVERSE_LAST_WORD:
MOV BX, CX   ; Store word length in BX
SUB SI, CX   ; Move SI back to start of word
REVERSE_LAST_LOOP:
MOV AL, [SI]
MOV [DI], AL
INC SI
DEC CX
INC DI
CMP CX, 0
JNE REVERSE_LAST_LOOP
MOV BYTE PTR [DI], 0   ; Null terminator
HLT          ; Halt the program
```

Count Number of Words in a Sentence

```
ORG 100h     ; Origin, start at address 100h
MOV SI, 200h  ; Start address of the string
```

```
MOV CX, 0    ; Initialize word count to 0
MOV AL, ' '  ; Set AL to space character
; String data (null-terminated)
MOV BYTE PTR [SI], 'H'
MOV BYTE PTR [SI + 1], 'e'
MOV BYTE PTR [SI + 2], 'l'
MOV BYTE PTR [SI + 3], 'l'
MOV BYTE PTR [SI + 4], 'o'
MOV BYTE PTR [SI + 5], ' '
MOV BYTE PTR [SI + 6], 'W'
MOV BYTE PTR [SI + 7], 'o'
MOV BYTE PTR [SI + 8], 'r'
MOV BYTE PTR [SI + 9], 'l'
MOV BYTE PTR [SI + 10], 'd'
MOV BYTE PTR [SI + 11], 0   ; Null terminator
COUNT_WORDS:
MOV BL, [SI] ; Load character from string
CMP BL, 0    ; Check for null terminator
JE DONE
CMP BL, ' '  ; Check for space
JNE NEXT_CHAR
INC CX       ; Increment word count for space
NEXT_CHAR:
INC SI       ; Move to next character
JMP COUNT_WORDS
DONE:
; CX now contains the number of words in the string
HLT          ; Halt the program
```

Convert Decimal Number to Roman Numeral

```
ORG 100h     ; Origin, start at address 100h
MOV AX, 1987  ; Load the decimal number
MOV DI, 300h  ; Start address for storing the Roman numeral
CONVERT_ROMAN:
CMP AX, 1000
JL HUNDREDS
MOV BYTE PTR [DI], 'M'
ADD DI, 1
SUB AX, 1000
JMP CONVERT_ROMAN
HUNDREDS:
CMP AX, 900
JL FIVE_HUNDREDS
MOV BYTE PTR [DI], 'C'
ADD DI, 1
MOV BYTE PTR [DI], 'M'
ADD DI, 1
SUB AX, 900
JMP CONVERT_ROMAN
FIVE_HUNDREDS:
CMP AX, 500
JL HUNDRED_FOUR_HUNDRED
MOV BYTE PTR [DI], 'D'
ADD DI, 1
SUB AX, 500
JMP CONVERT_ROMAN
HUNDRED_FOUR_HUNDRED:
CMP AX, 400
```

```
JL HUNDREDS_LOOP
MOV BYTE PTR [DI], 'C'
ADD DI, 1
MOV BYTE PTR [DI], 'D'
ADD DI, 1
SUB AX, 400
JMP CONVERT_ROMAN
HUNDREDS_LOOP:
CMP AX, 100
JL FIFTIES
MOV BYTE PTR [DI], 'C'
ADD DI, 1
SUB AX, 100
JMP HUNDREDS_LOOP
FIFTIES:
CMP AX, 90
JL TEN_FIFTIES
MOV BYTE PTR [DI], 'X'
ADD DI, 1
MOV BYTE PTR [DI], 'C'
ADD DI, 1
SUB AX, 90
JMP CONVERT_ROMAN
TEN_FIFTIES:
CMP AX, 50
JL FORTIES
MOV BYTE PTR [DI], 'L'
ADD DI, 1
SUB AX, 50
```

```
JMP CONVERT_ROMAN
FORTIES:
CMP AX, 40
JL TENS
MOV BYTE PTR [DI], 'X'
ADD DI, 1
MOV BYTE PTR [DI], 'L'
ADD DI, 1
SUB AX, 40
JMP CONVERT_ROMAN
TENS:
CMP AX, 10
JL FIVES
MOV BYTE PTR [DI], 'X'
ADD DI, 1
SUB AX, 10
JMP TENS
FIVES:
CMP AX, 9
JL ONE_FIVES
MOV BYTE PTR [DI], 'I'
ADD DI, 1
MOV BYTE PTR [DI], 'X'
ADD DI, 1
SUB AX, 9
JMP CONVERT_ROMAN
ONE_FIVES:
CMP AX, 5
JL ONES
```

```
MOV BYTE PTR [DI], 'V'
ADD DI, 1
SUB AX, 5
JMP CONVERT_ROMAN
ONES:
CMP AX, 4
JL ONES_LOOP
MOV BYTE PTR [DI], 'I'
ADD DI, 1
MOV BYTE PTR [DI], 'V'
ADD DI, 1
SUB AX, 4
JMP CONVERT_ROMAN
ONES_LOOP:
CMP AX, 1
JL DONE
MOV BYTE PTR [DI], 'I'
ADD DI, 1
SUB AX, 1
JMP ONES_LOOP
DONE:
MOV BYTE PTR [DI], 0 ; Null terminate the Roman numeral
HLT         ; Halt the program
```

Calculate Body Mass Index (BMI)

```
; Program: Calculate Body Mass Index (BMI)
; This program calculates the BMI given weight in kilograms and height in meters.
ORG 100h    ; Origin, start at address 100h
MOV AX, 7000  ; Weight in kilograms (70.00 kg)
```

MOV BX, 175   ; Height in centimeters (1.75 m, represented as 175 for precision)
; Convert height to meters squared
MOV CX, BX   ; Copy height to CX
MUL BX   ; AX = BX * BX (height^2)
MOV BX, 10000 ; Scaling factor for meters squared
DIV BX   ; DX:AX / 10000, quotient in AX (height^2)
; Calculate BMI (BMI = weight / height^2)
MOV BX, AX   ; Move height^2 to BX
MOV AX, 7000 ; Reload weight
MUL WORD PTR [SCALE] ; Scale weight for division
DIV BX   ; DX:AX / height^2, quotient in AX
; AX now contains the BMI
HLT   ; Halt the program
SCALE DW 100 ; Scaling factor for weight

Temperature Conversion (Celsius to Fahrenheit)

ORG 100h   ; Origin, start at address 100h
MOV AX, 25   ; Load temperature in Celsius
; Convert Celsius to Fahrenheit (F = C * 9/5 + 32)
MOV BX, 9   ; Numerator of the fraction
MUL BX   ; AX = AX * 9
MOV BX, 5   ; Denominator of the fraction
DIV BX   ; AX = AX / 5
ADD AX, 32   ; Add 32 to the result
; AX now contains the temperature in Fahrenheit
HLT   ; Halt the program

Temperature Conversion (Fahrenheit to Celsius)

ORG 100h   ; Origin, start at address 100h

```
MOV AX, 77    ; Load temperature in Fahrenheit
; Convert Fahrenheit to Celsius (C = (F - 32) * 5/9)
SUB AX, 32    ; Subtract 32 from the temperature
MOV BX, 5     ; Numerator of the fraction
MUL BX        ; AX = AX * 5
MOV BX, 9     ; Denominator of the fraction
DIV BX        ; AX = AX / 9
; AX now contains the temperature in Celsius
HLT           ; Halt the program
```

Generate Random Numbers

```
ORG 100h      ; Origin, start at address 100h
MOV AX, 1234h ; Seed value
RANDOM_LOOP:
MOV BX, 75h   ; Multiplier
MUL BX        ; AX = AX * BX
ADD AX, 1     ; Add increment
MOV CX, 100   ; Modulus
DIV CX        ; Divide by modulus
MOV DL, AH    ; Move quotient to DL for display
MOV AH, 2     ; DOS function to display character
INT 21h       ; Call DOS interrupt
MOV AH, 2     ; Display a space for separation
MOV DL, ' '
INT 21h       ; Call DOS interrupt
LOOP RANDOM_LOOP ; Repeat to generate more numbers
HLT           ; Halt the program
```

Simulate Dice Roll

```
ORG 100h      ; Origin, start at address 100h
MOV AX, 1234h ; Seed value for the random number generator
ROLL_DICE:
MOV BX, 75h   ; Multiplier
MUL BX        ; AX = AX * BX
ADD AX, 1     ; Add increment
MOV CX, 6     ; Modulus (6 for dice roll)
DIV CX        ; Divide by modulus
ADD DL, 1     ; Ensure the result is between 1 and 6
ADD DL, '0'   ; Convert number to ASCII
MOV AH, 2     ; DOS function to display character
INT 21h       ; Call DOS interrupt
HLT           ; Halt the program
```

Simulate Coin Toss

```
ORG 100h      ; Origin, start at address 100h
MOV AX, 1234h ; Seed value for the random number generator
TOSS_COIN:
MOV BX, 75h   ; Multiplier
MUL BX        ; AX = AX * BX
ADD AX, 1     ; Add increment
MOV CX, 2     ; Modulus (2 for coin toss)
DIV CX        ; Divide by modulus
ADD DL, 'H'   ; Result will be 'H' for heads or 'I' for tails ('H' + 0 or 'H' + 1)
CMP DL, 'H'   ; Check if it's heads
JE DISPLAY_RESULT
MOV DL, 'T'   ; If not heads, it's tails
```

```
DISPLAY_RESULT:
MOV AH, 2    ; DOS function to display character
INT 21h      ; Call DOS interrupt
HLT          ; Halt the program
```

Leap Year Check

```
ORG 100h     ; Origin, start at address 100h
MOV AX, 2024  ; Load the year to check
; Check if year is divisible by 4
MOV BX, 4
XOR DX, DX   ; Clear DX for division
DIV BX       ; Divide AX by 4
CMP DX, 0
JNE NOT_LEAP_YEAR
; Check if year is divisible by 100
MOV AX, BX   ; Load the year again
MOV BX, 100
XOR DX, DX   ; Clear DX for division
DIV BX       ; Divide AX by 100
CMP DX, 0
JNE LEAP_YEAR
; Check if year is divisible by 400
MOV AX, BX   ; Load the year again
MOV BX, 400
XOR DX, DX   ; Clear DX for division
DIV BX       ; Divide AX by 400
CMP DX, 0
JNE NOT_LEAP_YEAR
LEAP_YEAR:
```

```
MOV DL, 'Y'   ; 'Y' for leap year
JMP DISPLAY_RESULT
NOT_LEAP_YEAR:
MOV DL, 'N'   ; 'N' for not a leap year
DISPLAY_RESULT:
MOV AH, 2    ; DOS function to display character
INT 21h      ; Call DOS interrupt
HLT          ; Halt the program
```

Display Current Date and Time

```
ORG 100h      ; Origin, start at address 100h
MOV AH, 2Ah   ; DOS function to get date
INT 21h       ; Call DOS interrupt
; CX = year, DH = month, DL = day
; Display date
MOV AH, 2     ; DOS function to display character
MOV AL, DH
ADD AL, 30h   ; Convert month to ASCII
INT 21h       ; Display month
MOV DL, '/'
INT 21h       ; Display '/'
MOV AL, DL
ADD AL, 30h   ; Convert day to ASCII
INT 21h       ; Display day
MOV DL, '/'
INT 21h       ; Display '/'
MOV AX, CX
CALL PRINT_WORD ; Display year
; Get and display time
```

```
MOV AH, 2Ch   ; DOS function to get time
INT 21h       ; Call DOS interrupt
; CH = hour, CL = minute, DH = second
; Display time
MOV AL, CH
ADD AL, 30h   ; Convert hour to ASCII
INT 21h       ; Display hour
MOV DL, ':'
INT 21h       ; Display ':'
MOV AL, CL
ADD AL, 30h   ; Convert minute to ASCII
INT 21h       ; Display minute
MOV DL, ':'
INT 21h       ; Display ':'
MOV AL, DH
ADD AL, 30h   ; Convert second to ASCII
INT 21h       ; Display second
HLT           ; Halt the program
PRINT_WORD:   ; Subroutine to print AX as a 4-digit decimal
PUSH AX
PUSH CX
MOV CX, 1000
MOV AL, 0
DIV CX
ADD AL, 30h
INT 21h
POP CX
POP AX
RET
```

Generate Calendar of a Month

```
ORG 100h      ; Origin, start at address 100h
MOV AL, 1     ; Starting day of the week (0=Sunday, 1=Monday, ..., 6=Saturday)
MOV BL, 31    ; Number of days in the month
MOV CX, 2024  ; Year
MOV SI, 0     ; Counter for days
; Print header
MOV DX, OFFSET HEADER
MOV AH, 09h
INT 21h
; Print leading spaces for the first day
MOV CL, AL
PRINT_SPACES:
CMP CL, 0
JE PRINT_DAYS
MOV DL, ''
MOV AH, 2
INT 21h
MOV DL, ''
INT 21h
DEC CL
JMP PRINT_SPACES
PRINT_DAYS:
; Print the days of the month
MOV DI, 1
PRINT_LOOP:
MOV DL, DI
ADD DL, 30h
MOV AH, 2
```

```
INT 21h
MOV DL, ' '
INT 21h
INC SI
INC DI
CMP SI, 7
JNE CONTINUE
MOV DL, 0Dh
INT 21h
MOV DL, 0Ah
INT 21h
MOV SI, 0
CONTINUE:
CMP DI, BL
JLE PRINT_LOOP
HLT          ; Halt the program
HEADER DB 'Sun Mon Tue Wed Thu Fri Sat', 0Dh, 0Ah, '$'
```

Convert 12-hour Time Format to 24-hour

```
ORG 100h      ; Origin, start at address 100h
MOV AL, 2     ; Hour in 12-hour format (example: 2 PM)
MOV BL, 1     ; PM indicator (0=AM, 1=PM)
; Convert to 24-hour format
CMP BL, 1
JNE CONVERT_AM
ADD AL, 12    ; Add 12 to convert PM to 24-hour format
CONVERT_AM:
MOV BL, AL    ; Store result in BL
HLT           ; Halt the program
```

Convert 24-hour Time Format to 12-hour

```
ORG 100h     ; Origin, start at address 100h
MOV AL, 14   ; Hour in 24-hour format (example: 14)
; Convert to 12-hour format
CMP AL, 12
JL AM_PM_CHECK
SUB AL, 12   ; Subtract 12 for PM hours
MOV BL, 'P'  ; Set PM indicator
AM_PM_CHECK:
CMP AL, 12
JNE CONVERTED
MOV AL, 12   ; 12 PM is 12 in 12-hour format
CONVERTED:
CMP BL, 'P'
JE IS_PM
MOV BL, 'A'  ; Set AM indicator
IS_PM:
MOV DL, AL   ; Store hour in DL for display
HLT          ; Halt the program
```

Display Day of the Week for Given Date

```
ORG 100h     ; Origin, start at address 100h
MOV AX, 2024 ; Year
MOV BX, 6    ; Month (June)
MOV CX, 15   ; Day
; Zeller's Congruence algorithm
MOV DX, BX
CMP DX, 2
JG NO_ADJUST
```

```
ADD AX, -1
ADD DX, 12
NO_ADJUST:
MOV BX, AX
MOV AX, DX
ADD AX, 13
MUL AX
SHR AX, 2
MOV SI, AX
MOV AX, 5
MUL BX
SHR AX, 1
MOV DI, AX
ADD SI, CX
ADD SI, DI
ADD SI, 5
MOV BX, AX
MOV AX, 4
MUL BX
SHR AX, 2
ADD SI, AX
MOV AX, SI
MOV BX, 7
DIV BX
MOV AX, DX
; AX now contains the day of the week (0=Saturday, 1=Sunday, ..., 6=Friday)
HLT        ; Halt the program
```

Find Day of Year for Given Date

```
ORG 100h     ; Origin, start at address 100h
MOV AX, 2024  ; Year
MOV BX, 6    ; Month (June)
MOV CX, 15   ; Day
; Calculate day of the year
MOV DI, 0    ; Day of year counter
; Days in each month (non-leap year)
DAYS_IN_MONTH DB 31, 28, 31, 30, 31, 30, 31, 31, 30, 31, 30, 31
; Check for leap year
MOV DX, 4
DIV DX
CMP DX, 0
JNE NON_LEAP_YEAR
; Adjust February for leap year
ADD BYTE PTR [DAYS_IN_MONTH + 1], 1
NON_LEAP_YEAR:
MOV SI, BX
CALCULATE_DOY:
DEC SI
JS ADD_DAYS
MOV DL, [DAYS_IN_MONTH + SI]
ADD DI, DX
JMP CALCULATE_DOY
ADD_DAYS:
ADD DI, CX
; DI now contains the day of the year
HLT          ; Halt the program
```

Calculate Age in Days

```
ORG 100h      ; Origin, start at address 100h
MOV AX, 2000  ; Birth year
MOV BX, 6     ; Birth month (June)
MOV CX, 15    ; Birth day
MOV DX, 2024  ; Current year
MOV SI, 6     ; Current month (June)
MOV DI, 15    ; Current day
; Days in each month (non-leap year)
DAYS_IN_MONTH DB 31, 28, 31, 30, 31, 30, 31, 31, 30, 31, 30, 31
; Check for leap year
MOV BX, 4
DIV BX
CMP DX, 0
JNE NON_LEAP_YEAR
; Adjust February for leap year
ADD BYTE PTR [DAYS_IN_MONTH + 1], 1
NON_LEAP_YEAR:
; Calculate total days from birth year to current year
SUB DX, AX
MOV AX, DX
MUL WORD PTR [DAYS_IN_YEAR] ; Multiply by 365 (days in a year)
MOV DX, AX
; Add leap days
MOV BX, DX
SHR BX, 2
ADD DX, BX
; Add days from birth month to end of that year
MOV SI, 12
```

```
SUB SI, BX
MOV CX, BX
CALC_BIRTH_DAYS:
DEC SI
JS ADD_CURR_DAYS
MOV DL, [DAYS_IN_MONTH + SI]
ADD DX, DX
JMP CALC_BIRTH_DAYS
ADD_CURR_DAYS:
ADD DX, DX
; Add days from start of current year to current month
MOV BX, 0
CALC_CURR_DAYS:
MOV DL, [DAYS_IN_MONTH + BX]
ADD DX, DX
INC BX
CMP BX, SI
JL CALC_CURR_DAYS
ADD DX, DI
SUB DX, CX
; DX now contains the age in days
HLT          ; Halt the program
DAYS_IN_YEAR DW 365
```

Calculate Difference Between Two Dates

```
ORG 100h     ; Origin, start at address 100h
MOV AX, 2024 ; Year of first date
MOV BX, 6    ; Month of first date (June)
MOV CX, 15   ; Day of first date
```

```
MOV DX, 2024  ; Year of second date
MOV SI, 12    ; Month of second date (December)
MOV DI, 31    ; Day of second date
; Days in each month (non-leap year)
DAYS_IN_MONTH DB 31, 28, 31, 30, 31, 30, 31, 31, 30, 31, 30, 31
; Calculate days from first date to end of year
MOV BP, 0     ; Days counter
ADD_DAYS_FIRST:
MOV DL, [DAYS_IN_MONTH + BX - 1]
SUB DL, CL
ADD BP, DL
INC BX
CMP BX, 13
JNE ADD_DAYS_FIRST
; Calculate days from start of year to second date
MOV BX, 1
ADD_DAYS_SECOND:
MOV DL, [DAYS_IN_MONTH + BX - 1]
ADD BP, DL
INC BX
CMP BX, SI
JNE ADD_DAYS_SECOND
ADD BP, DI
; Calculate total years in between
SUB DX, AX
DEC DX
MUL DX, 365
; Add leap years
MOV AX, DX
```

SHR AX, 2

ADD BP, AX

; Add the days

ADD BP, AX

; BP now contains the difference in days

HLT   ; Halt the program

Convert Kilometers to Miles

ORG 100h   ; Origin, start at address 100h

MOV AX, 100   ; Distance in kilometers (example: 100 km)

; Convert kilometers to miles (1 km = 0.621371 miles)

MOV BX, 62137 ; Multiplier (0.621371 * 100000)

MUL BX   ; AX = AX * 62137

MOV BX, 100000 ; Scaling factor

DIV BX   ; DX:AX / 100000

; AX now contains the distance in miles

HLT   ; Halt the program

Convert Miles to Kilometers

ORG 100h   ; Origin, start at address 100h

MOV AX, 62   ; Distance in miles (example: 62 miles)

; Convert miles to kilometers (1 mile = 1.60934 km)

MOV BX, 160934 ; Multiplier (1.60934 * 100000)

MUL BX   ; AX = AX * 160934

MOV BX, 100000 ; Scaling factor

DIV BX   ; DX:AX / 100000

; AX now contains the distance in kilometers

HLT   ; Halt the program

Calculate Area of Circle

```
ORG 100h      ; Origin, start at address 100h
MOV AX, 10    ; Radius of the circle (example: 10 units)
; Calculate area (Area = π * r^2)
MUL AX        ; AX = r^2
MOV BX, 31416 ; Multiplier (π approximated to 3.1416 * 10000)
MUL BX        ; DX:AX = r^2 * π * 10000
MOV BX, 10000 ; Scaling factor
DIV BX        ; DX:AX / 10000
; AX now contains the area of the circle
HLT           ; Halt the program
```

Calculate Circumference of Circle

```
ORG 100h      ; Origin, start at address 100h
MOV AX, 10    ; Radius of the circle (example: 10 units)
; Calculate circumference (Circumference = 2 * π * r)
MOV BX, 62832 ; Multiplier (2 * π approximated to 6.2832 * 10000)
MUL BX        ; DX:AX = r * 2 * π * 10000
MOV BX, 10000 ; Scaling factor
DIV BX        ; DX:AX / 10000
; AX now contains the circumference of the circle
HLT           ; Halt the program
```

Calculate Area of Rectangle

```
ORG 100h      ; Origin, start at address 100h
MOV AX, 20    ; Length of the rectangle (example: 20 units)
MOV BX, 10    ; Width of the rectangle (example: 10 units)
; Calculate area (Area = Length * Width)
MUL BX        ; AX = AX * BX (Area = Length * Width)
```

```
; AX now contains the area of the rectangle

HLT         ; Halt the program
```

Calculate Perimeter of Rectangle

```
ORG 100h     ; Origin, start at address 100h

MOV AX, 20   ; Length of the rectangle (example: 20 units)

MOV BX, 10   ; Width of the rectangle (example: 10 units)

; Calculate perimeter (Perimeter = 2 * (Length + Width))

ADD AX, BX   ; AX = Length + Width

SHL AX, 1    ; AX = 2 * (Length + Width)

; AX now contains the perimeter of the rectangle

HLT          ; Halt the program
```

Calculate Area of Triangle

```
ORG 100h     ; Origin, start at address 100h

MOV AX, 10   ; Base of the triangle (example: 10 units)

MOV BX, 5    ; Height of the triangle (example: 5 units)

; Calculate area (Area = 0.5 * Base * Height)

MUL BX       ; AX = Base * Height

MOV BX, 2    ; Divisor for halving

DIV BX       ; AX = (Base * Height) / 2

; AX now contains the area of the triangle

HLT          ; Halt the program
```

Calculate Perimeter of Triangle

```
ORG 100h     ; Origin, start at address 100h

MOV AX, 10   ; Side 1 of the triangle (example: 10 units)

MOV BX, 8    ; Side 2 of the triangle (example: 8 units)

MOV CX, 6    ; Side 3 of the triangle (example: 6 units)
```

; Calculate perimeter (Perimeter = Side1 + Side2 + Side3)

ADD AX, BX   ; AX = Side1 + Side2

ADD AX, CX   ; AX = (Side1 + Side2) + Side3

; AX now contains the perimeter of the triangle

HLT   ; Halt the program

Calculate Volume of Sphere

ORG 100h   ; Origin, start at address 100h

MOV AX, 5   ; Radius of the sphere (example: 5 units)

; Calculate volume (Volume = 4/3 * π * r^3)

MOV BX, AX

MUL AX   ; AX = r^2

MUL BX   ; DX:AX = r^3

MOV BX, 4189 ; Multiplier (4/3 * π approximated to 4.18879 * 1000)

MUL BX   ; DX:AX = r^3 * 4189

MOV BX, 1000 ; Scaling factor

DIV BX   ; DX:AX / 1000

; AX now contains the volume of the sphere

HLT   ; Halt the program

Calculate Surface Area of Sphere

ORG 100h   ; Origin, start at address 100h

MOV AX, 5   ; Radius of the sphere (example: 5 units)

; Calculate surface area (Surface Area = 4 * π * r^2)

MUL AX   ; AX = r^2

MOV BX, 12566 ; Multiplier (4 * π approximated to 12.566 * 1000)

MUL BX   ; DX:AX = r^2 * 12566

MOV BX, 1000 ; Scaling factor

DIV BX   ; DX:AX / 1000

; AX now contains the surface area of the sphere

HLT   ; Halt the program

Calculate Volume of Cylinder

ORG 100h   ; Origin, start at address 100h

MOV AX, 5   ; Radius of the cylinder (example: 5 units)

MOV BX, 10   ; Height of the cylinder (example: 10 units)

; Calculate volume (Volume = π * r^2 * h)

MUL AX   ; AX = r^2

MOV CX, AX   ; Store r^2 in CX

MOV AX, BX   ; Load height into AX

MUL CX   ; AX = r^2 * h

MOV BX, 31416 ; Multiplier (π approximated to 3.1416 * 10000)

MUL BX   ; DX:AX = r^2 * h * π

MOV BX, 10000 ; Scaling factor

DIV BX   ; DX:AX / 10000

; AX now contains the volume of the cylinder

HLT   ; Halt the program

Calculate Surface Area of Cylinder

ORG 100h   ; Origin, start at address 100h

MOV AX, 5   ; Radius of the cylinder (example: 5 units)

MOV BX, 10   ; Height of the cylinder (example: 10 units)

; Calculate surface area (Surface Area = 2 * π * r * (r + h))

MOV CX, AX   ; Store radius in CX

ADD AX, BX   ; AX = r + h

MUL CX   ; AX = r * (r + h)

MOV BX, 62832 ; Multiplier (2 * π approximated to 6.2832 * 10000)

MUL BX   ; DX:AX = 2 * π * r * (r + h)

```
MOV BX, 10000 ; Scaling factor
DIV BX       ; DX:AX / 10000
; AX now contains the surface area of the cylinder
HLT          ; Halt the program
```

Calculate Volume of Cone

```
ORG 100h     ; Origin, start at address 100h
MOV AX, 5    ; Radius of the cone (example: 5 units)
MOV BX, 10   ; Height of the cone (example: 10 units)
; Calculate volume (Volume = 1/3 * π * r^2 * h)
MUL AX       ; AX = r^2
MOV CX, AX   ; Store r^2 in CX
MOV AX, BX   ; Load height into AX
MUL CX       ; AX = r^2 * h
MOV BX, 10472 ; Multiplier (1/3 * π approximated to 1.0472 * 10000)
MUL BX       ; DX:AX = r^2 * h * 1/3 * π
MOV BX, 10000 ; Scaling factor
DIV BX       ; DX:AX / 10000
; AX now contains the volume of the cone
HLT          ; Halt the program
```

Calculate Surface Area of Cone

```
ORG 100h     ; Origin, start at address 100h
MOV AX, 5    ; Radius of the cone (example: 5 units)
MOV BX, 12   ; Slant height of the cone (example: 12 units)
; Calculate surface area (Surface Area = π * r * (r + l))
ADD AX, BX   ; AX = r + l
MUL AX       ; AX = r * (r + l)
MOV BX, 31416 ; Multiplier (π approximated to 3.1416 * 10000)
```

```
MUL BX        ; DX:AX = π * r * (r + l) * 10000
MOV BX, 10000 ; Scaling factor
DIV BX        ; DX:AX / 10000
; AX now contains the surface area of the cone
HLT           ; Halt the program
```

Find Roots of Quadratic Equation

```
ORG 100h      ; Origin, start at address 100h
MOV AX, 1     ; Coefficient a (example: 1)
MOV BX, -3    ; Coefficient b (example: -3)
MOV CX, 2     ; Coefficient c (example: 2)
; Calculate discriminant (D = b^2 - 4ac)
MOV DX, BX    ; Load b into DX
IMUL DX, DX   ; DX = b^2
MOV SI, 4     ; Load 4 into SI
IMUL SI, AX   ; SI = 4a
IMUL SI, CX   ; SI = 4ac
SUB DX, SI    ; DX = b^2 - 4ac
; Check if discriminant is non-negative
JS NO_REAL_ROOTS
; Calculate root 1 (-b + sqrt(D)) / 2a
MOV SI, BX    ; Load b into SI
NEG SI        ; SI = -b
MOV CX, DX    ; Load discriminant into CX
CALL SQRT     ; Calculate sqrt(D)
ADD SI, AX    ; SI = -b + sqrt(D)
MOV AX, 2
IMUL AX, AX   ; AX = 2a
IDIV AX       ; AX = (-b + sqrt(D)) / 2a
```

```
MOV [ROOT1], AX
; Calculate root 2 (-b - sqrt(D)) / 2a
MOV SI, BX    ; Load b into SI
NEG SI        ; SI = -b
MOV CX, DX    ; Load discriminant into CX
CALL SQRT     ; Calculate sqrt(D)
SUB SI, AX    ; SI = -b - sqrt(D)
MOV AX, 2
IMUL AX, AX   ; AX = 2a
IDIV AX       ; AX = (-b - sqrt(D)) / 2a
MOV [ROOT2], AX
NO_REAL_ROOTS:
HLT           ; Halt the program
SQRT:
; Calculate the integer square root of CX (sqrt(D))
MOV AX, CX
MOV BX, 0
MOV DX, 0
SQRT_LOOP:
ADD DX, 1
IMUL DX, DX
CMP DX, AX
JLE SQRT_LOOP
SUB DX, 1
RET
ROOT1 DW 0
ROOT2 DW 0
```

Calculate Sine of Angle

```
ORG 100h     ; Origin, start at address 100h
MOV AX, 30   ; Angle in degrees (example: 30 degrees)
CALL DEG_TO_RAD ; Convert degrees to radians
; Calculate sine using x - x^3/3!
MOV BX, AX   ; Store x (radians) in BX
MUL AX       ; AX = x^2
MOV CX, AX   ; Store x^2 in CX
MUL BX       ; AX = x^3
MOV BX, 6    ; Denominator 3!
DIV BX       ; AX = x^3 / 6
SUB BX, AX   ; BX = x - (x^3 / 6)
; BX now contains the approximate value of sin(x)
HLT          ; Halt the program
DEG_TO_RAD:
; Convert degrees to radians (radians = degrees * π / 180)
MOV BX, 31416 ; π approximated to 3.1416 * 10000
MUL BX       ; AX = degrees * π * 10000
MOV BX, 180000 ; 180 * 1000 (scaling factor)
DIV BX       ; AX = degrees * π / 180
RET
```

Calculate Cosine of Angle

```
ORG 100h     ; Origin, start at address 100h
MOV AX, 30   ; Angle in degrees (example: 30 degrees)
CALL DEG_TO_RAD ; Convert degrees to radians
; Calculate cosine using 1 - x^2/2!
MOV BX, AX   ; Store x (radians) in BX
MUL AX       ; AX = x^2
```

```
MOV CX, AX    ; Store x^2 in CX
MOV BX, 2     ; Denominator 2!
DIV BX        ; AX = x^2 / 2
MOV BX, 10000 ; Scaling factor for 1 (1 * 10000)
SUB BX, AX    ; BX = 1 - (x^2 / 2)
; BX now contains the approximate value of cos(x)
HLT           ; Halt the program
DEG_TO_RAD:
; Convert degrees to radians (radians = degrees * π / 180)
MOV BX, 31416 ; π approximated to 3.1416 * 10000
MUL BX        ; AX = degrees * π * 10000
MOV BX, 180000 ; 180 * 1000 (scaling factor)
DIV BX        ; AX = degrees * π / 180
RET
```

Calculate Tangent of Angle

```
ORG 100h      ; Origin, start at address 100h
MOV AX, 30    ; Angle in degrees (example: 30 degrees)
CALL DEG_TO_RAD ; Convert degrees to radians
; Calculate sine using x - x^3/3!
MOV BX, AX    ; Store x (radians) in BX
MUL AX        ; AX = x^2
MOV CX, AX    ; Store x^2 in CX
MUL BX        ; AX = x^3
MOV BX, 6     ; Denominator 3!
DIV BX        ; AX = x^3 / 6
SUB BX, AX    ; BX = x - (x^3 / 6)
MOV SI, BX    ; Store sin(x) in SI
```

```
; Calculate cosine using 1 - x^2/2!
MOV BX, CX    ; Load x^2 from CX
MOV CX, 2     ; Denominator 2!
DIV CX        ; AX = x^2 / 2
MOV CX, 10000 ; Scaling factor for 1 (1 * 10000)
SUB CX, AX    ; CX = 1 - (x^2 / 2)
MOV DI, CX    ; Store cos(x) in DI
; Calculate tangent (tan(x) = sin(x) / cos(x))
MOV AX, SI    ; Load sin(x) into AX
MOV BX, DI    ; Load cos(x) into BX
DIV BX        ; AX = sin(x) / cos(x)
; AX now contains the approximate value of tan(x)
HLT           ; Halt the program
DEG_TO_RAD:
; Convert degrees to radians (radians = degrees * π / 180)
MOV BX, 31416 ; π approximated to 3.1416 * 10000
MUL BX        ; AX = degrees * π * 10000
MOV BX, 180000 ; 180 * 1000 (scaling factor)
DIV BX        ; AX = degrees * π / 180
RET
```

Calculate Logarithm of Number

```
ORG 100h      ; Origin, start at address 100h
MOV AX, 1     ; Number (1 + x) where x is small (example: ln(1.1))
; Calculate ln(1 + x) using x - x^2/2 + x^3/3
MOV BX, AX    ; Store x in BX
MUL AX        ; AX = x^2
MOV CX, AX    ; Store x^2 in CX
MOV BX, 2     ; Denominator 2
```

DIV BX   ; AX = x^2 / 2

SUB BX, AX   ; BX = x - (x^2 / 2)

MOV AX, BX   ; Load BX into AX

MUL CX   ; AX = x^3

MOV BX, 3   ; Denominator 3

DIV BX   ; AX = x^3 / 3

ADD BX, AX   ; BX = x - (x^2 / 2) + (x^3 / 3)

; BX now contains the approximate value of ln(1 + x)

HLT   ; Halt the program

Calculate Exponential of Number

ORG 100h   ; Origin, start at address 100h

MOV AX, 1   ; Number (x) (example: e^1)

; Calculate e^x using 1 + x + x^2/2! + x^3/3!

MOV BX, AX   ; Store x in BX

MUL AX   ; AX = x^2

MOV CX, AX   ; Store x^2 in CX

MOV AX, 1   ; Load 1 into AX

ADD AX, BX   ; AX = 1 + x

MOV BX, 2   ; Denominator 2!

DIV BX   ; AX = x^2 / 2

ADD AX, CX   ; AX = 1 + x + (x^2 / 2)

MOV BX, AX   ; Load AX into BX

MOV AX, CX   ; Load x^2 into AX

MUL CX   ; AX = x^4

MOV BX, 6   ; Denominator 3!

DIV BX   ; AX = x^3 / 6

ADD AX, BX   ; AX = 1 + x + (x^2 / 2) + (x^3 / 6)

; AX now contains the approximate value of e^x

```
HLT          ; Halt the program
```

Calculate Absolute Value

```
ORG 100h     ; Origin, start at address 100h
MOV AX, -1234 ; Load the number (example: -1234)
; Calculate absolute value
CMP AX, 0    ; Compare with zero
JGE POSITIVE  ; Jump if greater or equal (already positive)
NEG AX       ; Negate the value to make it positive
POSITIVE:
; AX now contains the absolute value of the number
HLT          ; Halt the program
```

Find Hamming Distance Between Two Strings

```
ORG 100h     ; Origin, start at address 100h
MOV SI, 200h ; Start address of first string
MOV DI, 300h ; Start address of second string
MOV CX, 10   ; Length of the strings
MOV DX, 0    ; Initialize Hamming distance to 0
; First string
MOV BYTE PTR [SI], 'a'
MOV BYTE PTR [SI + 1], 'b'
MOV BYTE PTR [SI + 2], 'c'
MOV BYTE PTR [SI + 3], 'd'
MOV BYTE PTR [SI + 4], 'e'
MOV BYTE PTR [SI + 5], 'f'
MOV BYTE PTR [SI + 6], 'g'
MOV BYTE PTR [SI + 7], 'h'
MOV BYTE PTR [SI + 8], 'i'
```

MOV BYTE PTR [SI + 9], 'j'

; Second string

MOV BYTE PTR [DI], 'a'

MOV BYTE PTR [DI + 1], 'b'

MOV BYTE PTR [DI + 2], 'x'

MOV BYTE PTR [DI + 3], 'd'

MOV BYTE PTR [DI + 4], 'y'

MOV BYTE PTR [DI + 5], 'f'

MOV BYTE PTR [DI + 6], 'g'

MOV BYTE PTR [DI + 7], 'z'

MOV BYTE PTR [DI + 8], 'i'

MOV BYTE PTR [DI + 9], 'j'

HAMMING_LOOP:

MOV AL, [SI] ; Load character from first string

MOV BL, [DI] ; Load character from second string

CMP AL, BL   ; Compare characters

JE CONTINUE   ; If equal, continue to next character

INC DX   ; If different, increment Hamming distance

CONTINUE:

INC SI   ; Move to next character in first string

INC DI   ; Move to next character in second string

LOOP HAMMING_LOOP ; Repeat for all characters

; DX now contains the Hamming distance

HLT   ; Halt the program

Check for Substring

ORG 100h   ; Origin, start at address 100h

MOV SI, 200h ; Start address of main string

MOV DI, 300h ; Start address of substring

```
MOV CX, 0     ; Initialize substring index
MOV DX, 0     ; Initialize match flag
; Main string
MOV BYTE PTR [SI], 'h'
MOV BYTE PTR [SI + 1], 'e'
MOV BYTE PTR [SI + 2], 'l'
MOV BYTE PTR [SI + 3], 'l'
MOV BYTE PTR [SI + 4], 'o'
MOV BYTE PTR [SI + 5], 0   ; Null terminator
; Substring
MOV BYTE PTR [DI], 'e'
MOV BYTE PTR [DI + 1], 'l'
MOV BYTE PTR [DI + 2], 'l'
MOV BYTE PTR [DI + 3], 0   ; Null terminator
CHECK_SUBSTRING:
MOV AL, [SI + CX] ; Load character from main string
CMP AL, 0        ; Check for null terminator
JE DONE
MOV BL, [DI + DX] ; Load character from substring
CMP BL, 0         ; Check for end of substring
JE FOUND
CMP AL, BL        ; Compare characters
JNE RESET         ; If not equal, reset substring index
INC DX            ; Increment substring index
JMP CONTINUE
RESET:
MOV DX, 0         ; Reset substring index
CONTINUE:
INC SI            ; Move to next character in main string
```

```
JMP CHECK_SUBSTRING
FOUND:
MOV DX, 1        ; Set match flag
DONE:
; DX now contains the match flag (1 if found, 0 if not)
HLT              ; Halt the program
```

String Concatenation

```
ORG 100h     ; Origin, start at address 100h
MOV SI, 200h  ; Start address of first string
MOV DI, 300h  ; Start address of second string
MOV BX, 400h  ; Start address of result string
; First string
MOV BYTE PTR [SI], 'h'
MOV BYTE PTR [SI + 1], 'e'
MOV BYTE PTR [SI + 2], 'l'
MOV BYTE PTR [SI + 3], 'l'
MOV BYTE PTR [SI + 4], 'o'
MOV BYTE PTR [SI + 5], 0   ; Null terminator
; Second string
MOV BYTE PTR [DI], ' '
MOV BYTE PTR [DI + 1], 'w'
MOV BYTE PTR [DI + 2], 'o'
MOV BYTE PTR [DI + 3], 'r'
MOV BYTE PTR [DI + 4], 'l'
MOV BYTE PTR [DI + 5], 'd'
MOV BYTE PTR [DI + 6], 0   ; Null terminator
; Copy first string to result
COPY_FIRST:
```

```
MOV AL, [SI]
CMP AL, 0
JE COPY_SECOND
MOV [BX], AL
INC SI
INC BX
JMP COPY_FIRST
; Copy second string to result
COPY_SECOND:
MOV AL, [DI]
CMP AL, 0
JE DONE
MOV [BX], AL
INC DI
INC BX
JMP COPY_SECOND
DONE:
MOV BYTE PTR [BX], 0 ; Null terminator
HLT          ; Halt the program
```

String Copy

```
ORG 100h     ; Origin, start at address 100h
MOV SI, 200h  ; Start address of source string
MOV DI, 300h  ; Start address of destination string
; Source string
MOV BYTE PTR [SI], 'h'
MOV BYTE PTR [SI + 1], 'e'
MOV BYTE PTR [SI + 2], 'l'
MOV BYTE PTR [SI + 3], 'l'
```

MOV BYTE PTR [SI + 4], 'o'

MOV BYTE PTR [SI + 5], 0   ; Null terminator

; Copy string

COPY_STRING:

MOV AL, [SI]

MOV [DI], AL

CMP AL, 0

JE DONE

INC SI

INC DI

JMP COPY_STRING

DONE:

HLT   ; Halt the program

String Compare

ORG 100h   ; Origin, start at address 100h

MOV SI, 200h ; Start address of first string

MOV DI, 300h ; Start address of second string

MOV DX, 0   ; Initialize compare result (0 = equal, 1 = not equal)

; First string

MOV BYTE PTR [SI], 'h'

MOV BYTE PTR [SI + 1], 'e'

MOV BYTE PTR [SI + 2], 'l'

MOV BYTE PTR [SI + 3], 'l'

MOV BYTE PTR [SI + 4], 'o'

MOV BYTE PTR [SI + 5], 0   ; Null terminator

; Second string

MOV BYTE PTR [DI], 'h'

MOV BYTE PTR [DI + 1], 'e'

```
MOV BYTE PTR [DI + 2], 'l'
MOV BYTE PTR [DI + 3], 'l'
MOV BYTE PTR [DI + 4], 'o'
MOV BYTE PTR [DI + 5], 0   ; Null terminator
COMPARE_STRING:
MOV AL, [SI]
MOV BL, [DI]
CMP AL, BL
JNE NOT_EQUAL
CMP AL, 0
JE DONE
INC SI
INC DI
JMP COMPARE_STRING
NOT_EQUAL:
MOV DX, 1    ; Set compare result to not equal
DONE:
; DX now contains the compare result (0 if equal, 1 if not equal)
HLT          ; Halt the program
```

Convert Integer to String

```
ORG 100h     ; Origin, start at address 100h
MOV AX, 12345 ; Integer to convert
MOV DI, 300h  ; Start address of result string
; Initialize variables
MOV CX, 10    ; Base 10 for division
MOV SI, DI    ; SI points to start of result string
; Convert integer to string
CONVERT_LOOP:
```

```
XOR DX, DX   ; Clear DX for DIV operation
DIV CX       ; Divide AX by 10, quotient in AX, remainder in DX
ADD DL, '0'  ; Convert remainder to ASCII digit
MOV [DI], DL ; Store ASCII digit in result string
INC DI       ; Move to next position in result string
CMP AX, 0    ; Check if AX (quotient) is 0
JNE CONVERT_LOOP ; If not zero, continue loop
; Reverse the string
MOV BX, DI   ; BX points to end of result string
DEC DI       ; Move DI back one position
REVERSE_LOOP:
CMP SI, DI   ; Compare SI (start) and DI (end)
JGE DONE_REV ; If SI >= DI, done reversing
MOV AL, [SI] ; Load character from start
MOV AH, [DI] ; Load character from end
MOV [SI], AH ; Swap characters
MOV [DI], AL
INC SI       ; Move SI forward
DEC DI       ; Move DI backward
JMP REVERSE_LOOP
DONE_REV:
; Null-terminate the string
MOV BYTE PTR [BX], 0 ; BX is the position after the last digit
HLT          ; Halt the program
```

Convert String to Integer

```
ORG 100h     ; Origin, start at address 100h
MOV SI, 300h ; Start address of string
MOV AX, 0    ; Initialize result
```

```
MOV CX, 10    ; Base 10
; Convert string to integer
CONVERT_LOOP:
MOV AL, [SI]  ; Load character from string
CMP AL, 0     ; Check for null terminator
JE DONE_CONV  ; If null terminator, done converting
SUB AL, '0'   ; Convert ASCII digit to value
MUL CX        ; AX = AX * 10
ADD AX, AL    ; AX = AX + AL
INC SI        ; Move to next character
JMP CONVERT_LOOP
DONE_CONV:
; AX now contains the integer representation of the string
HLT           ; Halt the program
```

Stack Operations (Push, Pop)

```
ORG 100h      ; Origin, start at address 100h
STACK_SIZE EQU 10 ; Size of the stack
MOV CX, 0     ; Initialize stack pointer (top of stack)
MOV SI, 200h  ; Start address of stack (adjust as needed)
MOV DI, 0     ; Temporarily used for data storage
; Push operation
PUSH_STACK:
CMP CX, STACK_SIZE ; Check if stack is full
JE STACK_FULL
MOV AX, 123   ; Example data to push onto stack
MOV [SI + CX], AX ; Push data onto stack
INC CX        ; Increment stack pointer
JMP POP_MENU  ; Go to menu for more operations
```

```
STACK_FULL:
MOV DX, OFFSET STACK_OVERFLOW_MSG ; Display overflow message
MOV AH, 09h
INT 21h
JMP POP_MENU
; Pop operation
POP_STACK:
CMP CX, 0     ; Check if stack is empty
JE STACK_EMPTY
DEC CX        ; Decrement stack pointer
MOV AX, [SI + CX] ; Pop data from stack
JMP POP_MENU   ; Go to menu for more operations
STACK_EMPTY:
MOV DX, OFFSET STACK_UNDERFLOW_MSG ; Display underflow message
MOV AH, 09h
INT 21h
JMP POP_MENU
; Menu for operations
POP_MENU:
MOV DX, OFFSET MENU_MSG
MOV AH, 09h
INT 21h
MOV AH, 01h    ; Read keypress
INT 21h
CMP AL, '1'    ; Check for push operation
JE PUSH_STACK
CMP AL, '2'    ; Check for pop operation
JE POP_STACK
HLT            ; Halt the program
```

; Data section

STACK_OVERFLOW_MSG DB "Stack Overflow!", 0Dh, 0Ah, '$'

STACK_UNDERFLOW_MSG DB "Stack Underflow!", 0Dh, 0Ah, '$'

MENU_MSG DB "1. Push to stack", 0Dh, 0Ah, "2. Pop from stack", 0Dh, 0Ah, "Enter choice: $"

Queue Operations (Enqueue, Dequeue)

ORG 100h   ; Origin, start at address 100h

QUEUE_SIZE EQU 10 ; Size of the queue

MOV CX, 0   ; Initialize queue pointer (front of queue)

MOV DX, 0   ; Initialize queue pointer (rear of queue)

MOV SI, 200h ; Start address of queue (adjust as needed)

MOV DI, 0   ; Temporarily used for data storage

; Enqueue operation

ENQUEUE_QUEUE:

CMP DX, QUEUE_SIZE ; Check if queue is full

JE QUEUE_FULL

MOV AX, 123   ; Example data to enqueue

MOV [SI + DX], AX ; Enqueue data

INC DX   ; Increment rear pointer

JMP DEQUEUE_MENU ; Go to menu for more operations

QUEUE_FULL:

MOV DX, OFFSET QUEUE_OVERFLOW_MSG ; Display overflow message

MOV AH, 09h

INT 21h

JMP DEQUEUE_MENU

; Dequeue operation

DEQUEUE_QUEUE:

CMP CX, DX   ; Check if queue is empty

JE QUEUE_EMPTY

```asm
MOV AX, [SI + CX] ; Dequeue data
INC CX          ; Increment front pointer
JMP DEQUEUE_MENU ; Go to menu for more operations
QUEUE_EMPTY:
MOV DX, OFFSET QUEUE_UNDERFLOW_MSG ; Display underflow message
MOV AH, 09h
INT 21h
JMP DEQUEUE_MENU
; Menu for operations
DEQUEUE_MENU:
MOV DX, OFFSET QUEUE_MENU_MSG
MOV AH, 09h
INT 21h
MOV AH, 01h    ; Read keypress
INT 21h
CMP AL, '1'    ; Check for enqueue operation
JE ENQUEUE_QUEUE
CMP AL, '2'    ; Check for dequeue operation
JE DEQUEUE_QUEUE
HLT            ; Halt the program
; Data section
QUEUE_OVERFLOW_MSG DB "Queue Overflow!", 0Dh, 0Ah, '$'
QUEUE_UNDERFLOW_MSG DB "Queue Underflow!", 0Dh, 0Ah, '$'
QUEUE_MENU_MSG DB "1. Enqueue to queue", 0Dh, 0Ah, "2. Dequeue from queue", 0Dh, 0Ah, "Enter choice: $"
```

Circular Queue

```asm
ORG 100h     ; Origin, start at address 100h
QUEUE_SIZE EQU 10 ; Size of the circular queue
```

```
MOV CX, 0    ; Initialize queue pointer (front of queue)
MOV DX, 0    ; Initialize queue pointer (rear of queue)
MOV SI, 200h  ; Start address of circular queue (adjust as needed)
MOV DI, 0    ; Temporarily used for data storage
; Enqueue operation
ENQUEUE_CIRCULAR_QUEUE:
MOV BX, DX    ; Save current rear pointer
INC DX        ; Increment rear pointer
MOV AX, 123   ; Example data to enqueue
MOV [SI + BX], AX ; Enqueue data
CMP DX, QUEUE_SIZE ; Check if rear pointer exceeds queue size
JB NO_WRAP    ; If not, skip wrap around
MOV DX, 0     ; Wrap rear pointer to start of queue
NO_WRAP:
JMP CIRCULAR_DEQUEUE_MENU ; Go to menu for more operations
; Dequeue operation
DEQUEUE_CIRCULAR_QUEUE:
CMP CX, DX    ; Check if queue is empty
JE CIRCULAR_QUEUE_EMPTY
MOV AX, [SI + CX] ; Dequeue data
INC CX        ; Increment front pointer
CMP CX, QUEUE_SIZE ; Check if front pointer exceeds queue size
JB NO_WRAP_FRONT ; If not, skip wrap around
MOV CX, 0     ; Wrap front pointer to start of queue
NO_WRAP_FRONT:
JMP CIRCULAR_DEQUEUE_MENU ; Go to menu for more operations
CIRCULAR_QUEUE_EMPTY:
MOV DX, OFFSET CIRCULAR_QUEUE_UNDERFLOW_MSG ; Display underflow message
MOV AH, 09h
```

INT 21h

JMP CIRCULAR_DEQUEUE_MENU

; Menu for operations

CIRCULAR_DEQUEUE_MENU:

MOV DX, OFFSET CIRCULAR_QUEUE_MENU_MSG

MOV AH, 09h

INT 21h

MOV AH, 01h   ; Read keypress

INT 21h

CMP AL, '1'   ; Check for enqueue operation

JE ENQUEUE_CIRCULAR_QUEUE

CMP AL, '2'   ; Check for dequeue operation

JE DEQUEUE_CIRCULAR_QUEUE

HLT   ; Halt the program

; Data section

CIRCULAR_QUEUE_UNDERFLOW_MSG DB "Circular Queue Underflow!", 0Dh, 0Ah, '$'

CIRCULAR_QUEUE_MENU_MSG DB "1. Enqueue to circular queue", 0Dh, 0Ah, "2. Dequeue from circular queue", 0Dh, 0Ah, "Enter choice: $"

Priority Queue

ORG 100h   ; Origin, start at address 100h

QUEUE_SIZE EQU 10 ; Size of the priority queue

MOV CX, 0   ; Initialize queue pointer (front of queue)

MOV DX, 0   ; Initialize queue pointer (rear of queue)

MOV SI, 200h ; Start address of priority queue (adjust as needed)

MOV DI, 0   ; Temporarily used for data storage

; Enqueue operation (assuming higher number = higher priority)

ENQUEUE_PRIORITY_QUEUE:

MOV BX, DX   ; Save current rear pointer

```asm
INC DX          ; Increment rear pointer
MOV AX, 123     ; Example data to enqueue
MOV [SI + BX], AX ; Enqueue data
; Sort queue based on priority (not implemented in this simplified example)
JMP PRIORITY_DEQUEUE_MENU ; Go to menu for more operations
; Dequeue operation
DEQUEUE_PRIORITY_QUEUE:
CMP CX, DX      ; Check if queue is empty
JE PRIORITY_QUEUE_EMPTY
MOV AX, [SI + CX] ; Dequeue data
INC CX          ; Increment front pointer
JMP PRIORITY_DEQUEUE_MENU ; Go to menu for more operations
PRIORITY_QUEUE_EMPTY:
MOV DX, OFFSET PRIORITY_QUEUE_UNDERFLOW_MSG ; Display underflow message
MOV AH, 09h
INT 21h
JMP PRIORITY_DEQUEUE_MENU
; Menu for operations
PRIORITY_DEQUEUE_MENU:
MOV DX, OFFSET PRIORITY_QUEUE_MENU_MSG
MOV AH, 09h
INT 21h
MOV AH, 01h     ; Read keypress
INT 21h
CMP AL, '1'     ; Check for enqueue operation
JE ENQUEUE_PRIORITY_QUEUE
CMP AL, '2'     ; Check for dequeue operation
JE DEQUEUE_PRIORITY_QUEUE
HLT             ; Halt the program
```

; Data section

PRIORITY_QUEUE_UNDERFLOW_MSG DB "Priority Queue Underflow!", 0Dh, 0Ah, '$'

PRIORITY_QUEUE_MENU_MSG DB "1. Enqueue to priority queue", 0Dh, 0Ah, "2. Dequeue from priority queue", 0Dh, 0Ah, "Enter choice: $"

Linked List (Insertion, Deletion)

ORG 100h   ; Origin, start at address 100h

; Node structure definition

NODE STRUCT

   DATA DW ?

   NEXT DW ?

NODE ENDS

; Initialize linked list head

MOV SI, 0   ; Start address of linked list head (adjust as needed)

MOV DI, 200h ; Start address of memory pool for nodes (adjust as needed)

MOV BX, DI   ; BX points to start of memory pool

; Insertion operation

INSERT_NODE:

MOV AX, 123   ; Example data to insert

MOV [DI].DATA, AX ; Store data in current node

MOV AX, SI   ; Store current head address in AX

MOV [DI].NEXT, AX ; Link current node to current head

MOV SI, DI   ; Update head to current node

ADD DI, SIZEOF NODE ; Move to next node in memory pool

JMP LINKED_LIST_MENU ; Go to menu for more operations

; Deletion operation

DELETE_NODE:

CMP SI, 0   ; Check if linked list is empty

JE LINKED_LIST_EMPTY

```
MOV AX, [SI].NEXT ; Get next node address
MOV SI, AX    ; Update head to next node
JMP LINKED_LIST_MENU ; Go to menu for more operations
LINKED_LIST_EMPTY:
MOV DX, OFFSET LINKED_LIST_UNDERFLOW_MSG ; Display underflow message
MOV AH, 09h
INT 21h
JMP LINKED_LIST_MENU
; Menu for operations
LINKED_LIST_MENU:
MOV DX, OFFSET LINKED_LIST_MENU_MSG
MOV AH, 09h
INT 21h
MOV AH, 01h    ; Read keypress
INT 21h
CMP AL, '1'    ; Check for insertion operation
JE INSERT_NODE
CMP AL, '2'    ; Check for deletion operation
JE DELETE_NODE
HLT            ; Halt the program
; Data section
LINKED_LIST_UNDERFLOW_MSG DB "Linked List Underflow!", 0Dh, 0Ah, '$'
LINKED_LIST_MENU_MSG DB "1. Insert into linked list", 0Dh, 0Ah, "2. Delete from linked list",
0Dh, 0Ah, "Enter choice: $"
```

Doubly Linked List

```
ORG 100h      ; Origin, start at address 100h
; Node structure definition
NODE STRUCT
```

```asm
    DATA DW ?
    PREV DW ?
    NEXT DW ?
NODE ENDS
; Initialize doubly linked list head and tail
MOV SI, 0    ; Start address of head (adjust as needed)
MOV DI, 200h  ; Start address of memory pool for nodes (adjust as needed)
MOV BX, DI   ; BX points to start of memory pool
; Insertion operation at head
INSERT_HEAD:
MOV AX, 123   ; Example data to insert
MOV [DI].DATA, AX ; Store data in current node
MOV AX, SI   ; Store current head address in AX
MOV [DI].NEXT, AX ; Link current node to current head
MOV [SI].PREV, DI ; Link current head's previous to current node
MOV SI, DI   ; Update head to current node
ADD DI, SIZEOF NODE ; Move to next node in memory pool
JMP DLL_MENU  ; Go to menu for more operations
; Deletion operation at head
DELETE_HEAD:
CMP SI, 0    ; Check if list is empty
JE DLL_EMPTY
MOV AX, [SI].NEXT ; Get next node address
MOV [AX].PREV, 0 ; Update new head's previous to NULL
MOV SI, AX   ; Update head to next node
JMP DLL_MENU  ; Go to menu for more operations
DLL_EMPTY:
MOV DX, OFFSET DLL_UNDERFLOW_MSG ; Display underflow message
MOV AH, 09h
```

```
INT 21h
JMP DLL_MENU
; Menu for operations
DLL_MENU:
MOV DX, OFFSET DLL_MENU_MSG
MOV AH, 09h
INT 21h
MOV AH, 01h   ; Read keypress
INT 21h
CMP AL, '1'   ; Check for insertion at head operation
JE INSERT_HEAD
CMP AL, '2'   ; Check for deletion at head operation
JE DELETE_HEAD
HLT           ; Halt the program
; Data section
DLL_UNDERFLOW_MSG DB "Doubly Linked List Underflow!", 0Dh, 0Ah, '$'
DLL_MENU_MSG DB "1. Insert at head", 0Dh, 0Ah, "2. Delete from head", 0Dh, 0Ah, "Enter
choice: $"
```

Circular Linked List

```
ORG 100h     ; Origin, start at address 100h
; Node structure definition
NODE STRUCT
   DATA DW ?
   NEXT DW ?
NODE ENDS
; Initialize circular linked list head
MOV SI, 0    ; Start address of head (adjust as needed)
MOV DI, 200h ; Start address of memory pool for nodes (adjust as needed)
```

```asm
MOV BX, DI    ; BX points to start of memory pool
; Insertion operation
INSERT_CIRCULAR:
MOV AX, 123    ; Example data to insert
MOV [DI].DATA, AX ; Store data in current node
MOV AX, SI    ; Store current head address in AX
MOV [DI].NEXT, AX ; Link current node to current head
MOV [BX].NEXT, DI ; Link last node to current node
MOV BX, DI    ; Update last node to current node
ADD DI, SIZEOF NODE ; Move to next node in memory pool
JMP CIRCULAR_MENU ; Go to menu for more operations
; Deletion operation
DELETE_CIRCULAR:
CMP SI, 0    ; Check if list is empty
JE CIRCULAR_EMPTY
MOV AX, [SI].NEXT ; Get next node address
MOV SI, AX    ; Update head to next node
MOV [BX].NEXT, SI ; Link last node to new head
JMP CIRCULAR_MENU ; Go to menu for more operations
CIRCULAR_EMPTY:
MOV DX, OFFSET CIRCULAR_UNDERFLOW_MSG ; Display underflow message
MOV AH, 09h
INT 21h
JMP CIRCULAR_MENU
; Menu for operations
CIRCULAR_MENU:
MOV DX, OFFSET CIRCULAR_MENU_MSG
MOV AH, 09h
INT 21h
```

```
MOV AH, 01h   ; Read keypress
INT 21h
CMP AL, '1'   ; Check for insertion operation
JE INSERT_CIRCULAR
CMP AL, '2'   ; Check for deletion operation
JE DELETE_CIRCULAR
HLT           ; Halt the program
; Data section
CIRCULAR_UNDERFLOW_MSG DB "Circular Linked List Underflow!", 0Dh, 0Ah, '$'
CIRCULAR_MENU_MSG DB "1. Insert into circular linked list", 0Dh, 0Ah, "2. Delete from
circular linked list", 0Dh, 0Ah, "Enter choice: $"
```

Binary Tree (Insertion, Traversal)

```
ORG 100h      ; Origin, start at address 100h
; Node structure definition
NODE STRUCT
   DATA DW ?
   LEFT DW ?
   RIGHT DW ?
NODE ENDS

; Initialize binary tree root
MOV SI, 0     ; Start address of root (adjust as needed)
MOV DI, 200h  ; Start address of memory pool for nodes (adjust as needed)
MOV BX, DI    ; BX points to start of memory pool
; Insertion operation
INSERT_BINARY_TREE:
MOV AX, 123   ; Example data to insert
MOV [DI].DATA, AX ; Store data in current node
```

```
MOV [DI].LEFT, 0 ; Initialize left child
MOV [DI].RIGHT, 0 ; Initialize right child
CMP SI, 0    ; Check if root is empty
JE ROOT_EMPTY
MOV CX, SI   ; Start from root
INSERT_LOOP:
MOV BX, CX   ; BX is parent node
MOV AX, [BX].DATA ; AX is parent data
CMP AX, [DI].DATA ; Compare with child data
JL INSERT_LEFT  ; If less, go left
JGE INSERT_RIGHT ; If greater or equal, go right
INSERT_LEFT:
MOV CX, [BX].LEFT ; Move left
CMP CX, 0    ; Check if empty
JNE INSERT_LOOP ; Not empty
MOV [BX].LEFT, DI ; Insert to left
JMP BINARY_MENU ; Menu
INSERT_RIGHT:
MOV CX, [BX].RIGHT ; Move right
CMP CX, 0    ; Check if empty
JNE INSERT_LOOP ; Not empty
MOV [BX].RIGHT, DI ; Insert to right
JMP BINARY_MENU ; Go to the menu for more operations
ROOT_EMPTY:
MOV SI, DI   ; Root to child
JMP BINARY_MENU ; Go to the menu for more operations
; Traversal operations (Preorder, Inorder, Postorder)
TRAVERSAL_BINARY_TREE:
MOV DX, OFFSET TRAVERSAL_MENU_MSG ; Display traversal menu
```

```
MOV AH, 09h
INT 21h
MOV AH, 01h    ; Read keypress
INT 21h
CMP AL, '1'    ; Preorder traversal
JE PREORDER_TRAVERSAL
CMP AL, '2'    ; Inorder traversal
JE INORDER_TRAVERSAL
CMP AL, '3'    ; Postorder traversal
JE POSTORDER_TRAVERSAL
JMP BINARY_MENU ; Go to the menu for more operations
PREORDER_TRAVERSAL:
MOV DX, OFFSET PREORDER_MSG ; Display "Preorder"
MOV AH, 09h
INT 21h
JMP BINARY_MENU ; Go to the menu for more operations
INORDER_TRAVERSAL:
MOV DX, OFFSET INORDER_MSG ; Display "Inorder"
MOV AH, 09h
INT 21h
JMP BINARY_MENU ; Go to the menu for more operations
POSTORDER_TRAVERSAL:
MOV DX, OFFSET POSTORDER_MSG ; Display "Postorder"
MOV AH, 09h
INT 21h
JMP BINARY_MENU ; Go to the menu for more operations
; Menu for operations
BINARY_MENU:
MOV DX, OFFSET BINARY_TREE_MENU_MSG
```

```asm
MOV AH, 09h
INT 21h
MOV AH, 01h    ; Read keypress
INT 21h
CMP AL, '1'   ; Insertion operation
JE INSERT_BINARY_TREE
CMP AL, '2'    ; Traversal operation
JE TRAVERSAL_BINARY_TREE
HLT           ; Halt the program
; Data section
BINARY_TREE_MENU_MSG DB "1. Insert into binary tree", 0Dh, 0Ah, "2. Traverse binary tree", 0Dh, 0Ah, "Enter choice: $"
TRAVERSAL_MENU_MSG DB "Binary Tree Traversal:", 0Dh, 0Ah, "1. Preorder", 0Dh, 0Ah, "2. Inorder", 0Dh, 0Ah, "3. Postorder", 0Dh, 0Ah, "Enter choice: $"
PREORDER_MSG DB "Preorder traversal", 0Dh, 0Ah, '$'
INORDER_MSG DB "Inorder traversal", 0Dh, 0Ah, '$'
POSTORDER_MSG DB "Postorder traversal", 0Dh, 0Ah, '$'
```

Implement Binary Search Tree

```asm
ORG 100h    ; Start address
; Define node structure
NODE STRUCT
   DATA DW ?
   LEFT DW ?
   RIGHT DW ?
NODE ENDS
; Constants
MAX_NODES equ 10    ; Maximum number of nodes
; Variables
```

```asm
root DW 0          ; Root of the Binary Search Tree
nodes_used DW 0    ; Count of nodes used
node_memory NODE MAX_NODES dup(?)   ; Memory pool for nodes
; Main program
MAIN:
   MOV ax, @data   ; Initialize data segment
   MOV ds, ax
   ; Display menu
   CALL DISPLAY_MENU
   ; Handle user input
   MOV ah, 01h     ; Read character from keyboard
   INT 21h         ; DOS interrupt
   CMP al, '1'     ; Insertion operation
   JE INSERT_NODE
   CMP al, '2'     ; Inorder traversal
   JE INORDER_TRAVERSAL
   CMP al, '3'     ; Exit
   JE EXIT_PROGRAM
   JMP MAIN        ; Repeat main loop
; Function to display menu
DISPLAY_MENU:
   MOV dx, OFFSET MENU_TEXT
   MOV ah, 09h     ; DOS function to display string
   INT 21h
   RET
; Function to insert a node into BST
INSERT_NODE:
   ; Check if maximum nodes reached
   CMP nodes_used, MAX_NODES
```

```
JE BST_FULL
; Read input data
MOV dx, OFFSET ENTER_DATA_TEXT
MOV ah, 09h
INT 21h
; Read integer input
MOV ah, 01h    ; Read character from keyboard
INT 21h        ; DOS interrupt
SUB al, 30h    ; Convert ASCII to integer
MOV bx, ax     ; Store data in bx
; Initialize node with input data
MOV di, node_memory
ADD di, nodes_used
MOV [di].DATA, bx   ; Store data in node
MOV [di].LEFT, 0    ; Initialize left child
MOV [di].RIGHT, 0   ; Initialize right child
; Insert node into BST
CMP nodes_used, 0   ; Check if tree is empty
JE INSERT_ROOT
MOV si, root        ; Start from root
INSERT_LOOP:
   MOV bx, si    ; bx is current node
   MOV ax, [bx].DATA   ; ax is data in current node
   CMP bx, di    ; Compare current node with new node
   JL INSERT_LEFT ; If less, go left
   JGE INSERT_RIGHT ; If greater or equal, go right
INSERT_LEFT:
   MOV si, [bx].LEFT   ; Move to left child
   CMP si, 0      ; Check if left child is empty
```

```
    JNE INSERT_LOOP     ; Not empty, continue insertion loop
    MOV [bx].LEFT, di   ; Insert new node as left child
    JMP INSERT_END
  INSERT_RIGHT:
    MOV si, [bx].RIGHT  ; Move to right child
    CMP si, 0       ; Check if right child is empty
    JNE INSERT_LOOP     ; Not empty, continue insertion loop
    MOV [bx].RIGHT, di  ; Insert new node as right child
    JMP INSERT_END
  INSERT_ROOT:
    MOV root, di    ; Set new node as root
  INSERT_END:
    INC nodes_used  ; Increment count of used nodes
    JMP MAIN        ; Return to main menu
BST_FULL:
  MOV dx, OFFSET BST_FULL_TEXT
  MOV ah, 09h
  INT 21h
  JMP MAIN        ; Return to main menu
; Function to perform inorder traversal of BST
INORDER_TRAVERSAL:
  CMP nodes_used, 0   ; Check if tree is empty
  JE BST_EMPTY
  MOV dx, OFFSET INORDER_TEXT
  MOV ah, 09h
  INT 21h
  MOV si, root        ; Start from root
  CALL INORDER        ; Perform inorder traversal
  JMP MAIN        ; Return to main menu
```

```asm
INORDER:
    CMP si, 0       ; Check if current node is empty
    JE INORDER_END
    ; Traverse left subtree
    MOV bx, si      ; bx is current node
    MOV si, [bx].LEFT   ; Move to left child
    CALL INORDER        ; Recursively traverse left subtree
    ; Print current node data
    MOV bx, si      ; bx is current node
    MOV ax, [bx].DATA   ; ax is data in current node
    ADD ax, 30h     ; Convert integer to ASCII
    MOV dl, al      ; dl is ASCII character to display
    MOV ah, 02h     ; DOS function to display character
    INT 21h
    ; Traverse right subtree
    MOV bx, si      ; bx is current node
    MOV si, [bx].RIGHT  ; Move to right child
    CALL INORDER        ; Recursively traverse right subtree
INORDER_END:
    RET
BST_EMPTY:
    MOV dx, OFFSET BST_EMPTY_TEXT
    MOV ah, 09h
    INT 21h
    JMP MAIN        ; Return to main menu
EXIT_PROGRAM:
    MOV ah, 4Ch     ; DOS function to terminate program
    INT 21h
    RET
```

```
; Data section
MENU_TEXT DB 0Dh, 0Ah, "Binary Search Tree Operations:", 0Dh, 0Ah
        DB "1. Insert node", 0Dh, 0Ah
        DB "2. Inorder traversal", 0Dh, 0Ah
        DB "3. Exit", 0Dh, 0Ah
        DB "Enter choice: $"
ENTER_DATA_TEXT DB 0Dh, 0Ah, "Enter integer data to insert: $"
BST_FULL_TEXT DB 0Dh, 0Ah, "Binary Search Tree is full!", 0Dh, 0Ah, '$'
INORDER_TEXT DB 0Dh, 0Ah, "Inorder traversal:", 0Dh, 0Ah, '$'
BST_EMPTY_TEXT DB 0Dh, 0Ah, "Binary Search Tree is empty!", 0Dh, 0Ah, '$'
```

Implement AVL Tree

```
ORG 100h     ; Origin, start at address 100h
; Node structure definition
NODE STRUCT
   DATA DW ?
   LEFT DW ?
   RIGHT DW ?
   HEIGHT DW ?
NODE ENDS
; Initialize AVL tree root
MOV SI, 0    ; Start address of root (adjust as needed)
MOV DI, 200h  ; Start address of memory pool for nodes (adjust as needed)
MOV BX, DI    ; BX points to start of memory pool
; Insertion operation
INSERT_AVL:
MOV AX, 123    ; Example data to insert
MOV [DI].DATA, AX ; Store data in current node
MOV [DI].LEFT, 0 ; Initialize left child
```

```asm
MOV [DI].RIGHT, 0 ; Initialize right child
MOV [DI].HEIGHT, 1 ; Initialize height
CMP SI, 0     ; Check if root is empty
JE ROOT_EMPTY_AVL
MOV CX, SI    ; Start from root
INSERT_LOOP_AVL:
MOV BX, CX    ; BX is parent node
MOV AX, [BX].DATA ; AX is parent data
CMP AX, [DI].DATA ; Compare with child data
JL INSERT_LEFT_AVL ; If less, go left
JGE INSERT_RIGHT_AVL ; If greater or equal, go right
INSERT_LEFT_AVL:
MOV CX, [BX].LEFT ; Move left
CMP CX, 0     ; Check if empty
JNE INSERT_LOOP_AVL ; Not empty
MOV [BX].LEFT, DI ; Insert to left
CALL BALANCE_AVL ; Balance AVL tree
JMP AVL_MENU  ; Go to menu for more operations
INSERT_RIGHT_AVL:
MOV CX, [BX].RIGHT ; Move right
CMP CX, 0     ; Check if empty
JNE INSERT_LOOP_AVL ; Not empty
MOV [BX].RIGHT, DI ; Insert to right
CALL BALANCE_AVL ; Balance AVL tree
JMP AVL_MENU  ; Go to menu for more operations
ROOT_EMPTY_AVL:
MOV SI, DI    ; Root to child
JMP AVL_MENU  ; Go to menu for more operations
; AVL tree balancing function
```

```
BALANCE_AVL:
; Implement AVL tree balancing algorithm here
RET
; Traversal operations (Inorder)
TRAVERSAL_AVL:
MOV DX, OFFSET INORDER_MSG_AVL ; Display inorder message
MOV AH, 09h
INT 21h
TRAVERSAL_LOOP_AVL:
MOV CX, SI    ; Start from root
TRAVERSE_INORDER_AVL:
CMP CX, 0     ; Check if empty
JE END_TRAVERSAL_AVL ; End traversal
MOV BX, CX    ; BX is parent node
MOV AX, [BX].LEFT ; AX is left child
CMP AX, 0     ; Compare with child
JE PRINT_AVL  ; Print child
TRAVERSE_INORDER_LOOP_AVL:
MOV CX, AX    ; Start from left child
JMP TRAVERSE_INORDER_AVL ; Go to the next operation
PRINT_AVL:
; Print node's data (implementation depends on requirements)
RET
END_TRAVERSAL_AVL:
RET
; Menu for operations
AVL_MENU:
MOV DX, OFFSET AVL_TREE_MENU_MSG
MOV AH, 09h
```

```
INT 21h

MOV AH, 01h    ; Read keypress

INT 21h

CMP AL, '1'    ; Insertion operation

JE INSERT_AVL

CMP AL, '2'    ; Traversal operation

JE TRAVERSAL_AVL

HLT            ; Halt the program

; Data section

AVL_TREE_MENU_MSG DB "1. Insert into AVL tree", 0Dh, 0Ah, "2. Traverse AVL tree", 0Dh,
0Ah, "Enter choice: $"

INORDER_MSG_AVL DB "Inorder traversal", 0Dh, 0Ah, '$'
```

Implement Graph (Adjacency Matrix)

```
ORG 100h       ; Origin, start at address 100h

MOV AX, 5      ; Number of vertices (adjust as needed)

MOV BX, AX     ; BX holds number of vertices

; Initialize adjacency matrix

MOV DI, 200h   ; Start address of adjacency matrix (adjust as needed)

MOV CX, 0      ; Initialize counter for rows

INITIALIZE_GRAPH:

MOV DX, DI     ; DX points to current row

MOV SI, 0      ; Initialize counter for columns

INITIALIZE_ROW:

MOV [DX + SI], 0 ; Initialize each element to 0 (no edge)

INC SI         ; Move to next column

CMP SI, BX     ; Check if all columns are initialized

JL INITIALIZE_ROW ; Repeat for all columns

ADD DI, BX     ; Move to next row
```

```asm
INC CX        ; Move to next row counter
CMP CX, BX    ; Check if all rows are initialized
JL INITIALIZE_GRAPH ; Repeat for all rows
; Add edges (example: add edge between vertex 1 and vertex 2)
MOV AX, 1     ; Source vertex (adjust as needed)
MOV DX, 2     ; Destination vertex (adjust as needed)
SUB AX, 1     ; Adjust for zero-based indexing
SUB DX, 1     ; Adjust for zero-based indexing
MOV SI, AX    ; SI holds source vertex index
MOV DI, DX    ; DI holds destination vertex index
MOV BX, BX    ; BX holds number of vertices
; Mark adjacency in matrix (assuming undirected graph)
MOV CX, 1     ; Set edge weight (1 for existence of edge)
MOV AX, SI    ; AX holds source vertex index
MUL BX        ; Multiply by number of vertices
ADD AX, DI    ; Add destination vertex index
MOV DX, AX    ; DX holds index in adjacency matrix
MOV [200h + DX], CX ; Mark adjacency in matrix
MOV [200h + DX], CX ; Mark adjacency in matrix
JMP GRAPH_MENU ; Go to menu for more operations
; Check if there is an edge between two vertices (example: between vertex 1 and vertex 2)
MOV AX, 1     ; Source vertex (adjust as needed)
MOV DX, 2     ; Destination vertex (adjust as needed)
SUB AX, 1     ; Adjust for zero-based indexing
SUB DX, 1     ; Adjust for zero-based indexing
MOV SI, AX    ; SI holds source vertex index
MOV DI, DX    ; DI holds destination vertex index
MOV BX, BX    ; BX holds number of vertices
; Check adjacency in matrix (assuming undirected graph)
```

```
MOV CX, 1      ; Set edge weight (1 for existence of edge)
MOV AX, SI     ; AX holds source vertex index
MUL BX         ; Multiply by number of vertices
ADD AX, DI     ; Add destination vertex index
MOV DX, AX     ; DX holds index in adjacency matrix
MOV [200h + DX], CX ; Check adjacency in matrix
MOV [200h + DX], CX ; Check adjacency in matrix
JMP GRAPH_MENU ; Go to menu for more operations
; Menu for operations
GRAPH_MENU:
MOV DX, OFFSET GRAPH_MENU_MSG
MOV AH, 09h
INT 21h
MOV AH, 01h    ; Read keypress
INT 21h
CMP AL, '1'    ; Add edge operation
JE ADD_EDGE
CMP AL, '2'    ; Check edge operation
JE CHECK_EDGE
HLT            ; Halt the program
; Data section
GRAPH_MENU_MSG DB "Graph Operations:", 0Dh, 0Ah, "1. Add edge", 0Dh, 0Ah, "2. Check
edge", 0Dh, 0Ah, "Enter choice: $"
```

www.ingramcontent.com/pod-product-compliance
Lightning Source LLC
LaVergne TN
LVHW020340200726

843507LV00012B/2430